MAIN

S0-AFE-417

WITHDRAWN

Ten-Minute Plays

VOLUME VI

FOR MIDDLE SCHOOL: COMEDY

10+ Format

Ten-Minute Plays

VOLUME VI

FOR MIDDLE SCHOOL

. . .

COMEDY

10+ Format

YOUNG ACTORS SERIES

Kristen Dabrowski

A Smith and Kraus

Orange Public Library
Orange, CA 92866
ODC - 2006

A Smith and Kraus Book
Published by Smith and Kraus, Inc.
177 Lyme Road, Hanover, NH 03755
www.SmithandKraus.com

© 2006 by Kristen Dabrowski
All rights reserved.

CAUTION: Professionals and amateurs are hereby warned that the plays represented in this book are subject to a royalty. They are fully protected under the copyright laws of the United States of America, and of all countries covered by the International Copyright Union (including the Dominion of Canada and the rest of the British Commonwealth), and of all countries covered by the Pan-American Copyright Convention and the Universal Copyright Convention, and of all countries with which the United States has reciprocal copyright relations. All rights, including professional, amateur, motion picture, recitation, lecturing, public reading, radio broadcasting, television, video or sound taping, all other forms of mechanical or electronic reproductions such as information storage and retrieval systems and photocopying, and the rights of translation into foreign languages, are strictly reserved. Inquiries concerning all rights should be addressed to Smith and Kraus, PO Box 127, Lyme, NH 03768; tel. (603) 643-6431.

First Edition: April 2006
10 9 8 7 6 5 4 3 2 1
Manufactured in the United States of America

Cover and text design by Julia Hill Gignoux, Freedom Hill Design

ISBN 1-57525-442-5
10-Minute Plays for Kids Series ISSN 1553-0477

CONTENTS

TO MARY KEMP, BETTY LIES,
AND WALTER DABROWSKI
for being inspiring teachers

INTRODUCTION

Ten-Minute Plays aims to score on many playing fields. This book contains twelve short plays. Each play then contains two scenes and four monologues. Add it up! That means that this book contains twelve plays, twenty-four scenes, and forty-eight monologues. There's a lot to choose from, but it's not overwhelming. The plays and scenes are marked clearly. Note that the text for the monologues is set in a different typeface. If you are working on a monologue and are not performing the play or scene as a whole, take the time to hear in your mind any additional lines or character responses that you need for the monologue to make sense.

Beat indicates there is a dramatic pause in the action. You will want to consider why the beat is there. Does no one know what to do? Is someone thinking?

Feel free to combine characters (so fewer actors are needed), change a character from male to female (or vice versa), or alter the text in any way that suits you. Be as creative as you like!

For each play, I've included tips for young actors and ideas for playwrights. Here's a guide to the symbols:

🎭 = tips for actors

🖊 = ideas for playwrights

There's a lot to work with here. Actors, the tips are meant to give you some guidance and information on how to be an even finer actor. Playwrights, I've included a few of my inspirations and invite you to borrow from them to write your own plays.

At the end of each play is a section called "Talk Back!" with discussion questions. These questions are catalysts for class discussions and projects. The plays do not make moral judgments. They are intended to spark students to use their imaginations and create their own code of ethics. Even if you're not in school, "Talk Back!" can give you some additional ideas and interesting subjects to discuss.

Lastly, there are four extras in the Appendix: Character Questionnaire for Actors, Playwright's Checklist, Scene Elements Worksheet, and Exploration Games. Each activity adds dimension and depth to the plays and is intended to appeal to various learning styles.

Enjoy!

Kristen Dabrowski

THE DIRECTOR

7F, 5M

WHO

FEMALES
> Danielle
> Denise
> Gia
> Kim
> Olivia
> Summer
> Tori

MALES
> Brad
> Ed
> Jud
> Miles
> Travis

WHERE Outside.

WHEN Present day.

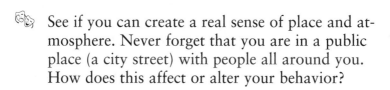 See if you can create a real sense of place and atmosphere. Never forget that you are in a public place (a city street) with people all around you. How does this affect or alter your behavior?

Many years ago, there was a TV show about a sixteenyear-old doctor. Write a play about a young character trying to work in an adult profession and the problems he or she faces.

Scene 1: Filming

MILES: OK. Look scary.

(*JUD, OLIVIA, and KIM make scary faces.*)

MILES: No! Less scary. More zombie-ish.

(*JUD, OLIVIA, and KIM look bored.*)

MILES: No. More scary!

KIM: But when we did more scary, you said to be less scary.

MILES: Somewhere between the two! Be scary, but be a zombie.

TORI: Listen, if this is going to take a while, can I go take a break and get something to drink?

JUD: If she gets to take a break, then I want one, too.

MILES: No one is going to take a break! Now, think about what it's like to be a zombie, people. You're brains have been eaten. And now you're hungry. Very, very hungry. You want Tori's brain. You want it more than you've ever wanted anything.

OLIVIA: Doesn't seem like much food for all three of us.

TORI: Are you saying I'm dumb?

OLIVIA: I'm just saying that one brain for three hungry zombies—

MILES: Well, that's all you've got. So, once again, you come after Tori, looking scary, because you want to eat her brain—

JUD: Olivia is right. We need two more girls to chase so there's enough brains for all of—

MILES: Just do it!

KIM: Take it easy, Miles. It's just a movie.

MILES: Just a movie? Just a movie? This is an important movie. This is *my* movie. This is a movie that is going to make me millions of dollars.

KIM: You really think so?

MILES: It's possible.

KIM: I don't mean to be cruel, but I doubt it.

MILES: It's possible! If only we'd all do what we're supposed to do!

TORI: OK, OK! Let's do it! I'm sick of waiting around.

MILES: OK. Places, everyone.

(KIM, TORI, JUD, and OLIVIA go to their places.)

MILES: Ready? And . . . action!

(KIM, JUD, and OLIVIA hold their arms out in front of them and slowly advance on TORI.)

TORI: No! No! Go away!

MILES: CUT!

OLIVIA: Don't tell me we weren't scary enough. I think I was being pretty scary.

MILES: No, no, it was fine.

JUD: What then?

MILES: Tori, your line is "No! Go away! No!"

TORI: That's what I said.

MILES: No. You said, "No! No! Go away!"

TORI: What's the difference?

MILES: The difference is that "go away" is said *between* the two "no's."

TORI: It seems the same to me.

JUD: Tori, just say it the other way, *please*. I want to finish this and go home.

OLIVIA: This was a lot more fun when we started.

KIM: *You* were a lot more fun when we started, Miles.

MILES: Me? I'm exactly the same.

KIM: No way.

MILES: Yes way. I just have to be a little . . . demanding so we get this done.

JUD: Fine, fine, fine. Let's go.

MILES: OK. Places.

(*OLIVIA, KIM, JUD, and TORI get in their places.*)

MILES: And . . . action!

(*KIM, JUD, and OLIVIA hold their arms out in front of them and slowly advance on TORI.*)

TORI: No! Go—

(*TRAVIS and GIA enter.*)

TRAVIS: What's going on?

MILES: Cut!

TRAVIS: You making a movie?

MILES: Yes, we're making a movie. What do you think we're doing?

GIA: I thought you were making a movie. Travis, we're in a movie!

TRAVIS: I always wanted to be in a movie.

GIA: I was born to be in a movie!

MILES: I'm sure you were, but maybe it's another movie. We've got to finish this one; I'd really appreciate it if you would clear the set.

TRAVIS: This isn't a set; it's a sidewalk!

MILES: Well, today it's a set. Do you mind?

GIA: Who do you think you are?

MILES: The director.

GIA: Oh. He's the director, Travis!

TRAVIS: I heard him.

JUD: Hey, would you want to get your brains eaten out by zombies?

GIA: In a movie or in real life?

JUD: In a mov—

MILES: Jud, this is *my* movie, not yours.

JUD: I just thought that they want to be in a movie, and that way we'd all get our own brains so we wouldn't have to share. I don't see zombies being really good at sharing.

GIA: Mister director, let me tell you what you've got here. I am a superstar. A one-hundred-percent, bona-fide superstar. I've got what they call the "it" factor. I don't know if you know what that is, so let me try to describe my awesomeness to you. I glow. I sparkle. I shine. I light up a room. I have a billion-watt smile. There isn't anyone else in the world like me. So if you want a zombie or whatever, I will give you the best zombie you have ever seen. You will think I never ever had a brain. I will walk slower than anyone else with my eyes rolled back in my head. Or, if you prefer, I will run from the zombies screaming. Can I ever scream! Just ask my brother. It's my secret weapon when he tries to read my diary. I scream and scream and scream like you wouldn't believe. So if you don't put me in your movie, you are one big fool.

MILES: Fine. You and your friend run from the zombies screaming. OK?

GIA: You got it.

TRAVIS: No problem. My name is Travis. T-R-A-V-I-S.

MILES: OK. Places! And . . . action!

TORI: No!

GIA: My God! Zombies! What are we going to do?

TORI: Wait a minute! I thought *I* had the lines in this scene.

MILES: Cut! Whatever! I don't even care anymore. Let's go! And . . . action!

TORI: *(Trying to speak over GIA.)* I've never been so scared in my life! Help! No!

GIA: *(Talking loudly at the same time as TORI.)* I'm not ready to have my brain eaten! Oh, help me, someone! I'm terrified!

TRAVIS: Help. I'm not kidding. I need help here. This is no joke.

MILES: Keep going!

KIM/JUD/OLIVIA: Grrrrr.

GIA: Aaaaaah!

(ED, DANIELLE, SUMMER, BRAD, and DENISE walk in front of KIM, OLIVIA, JUD, GIA, TRAVIS, and TORI.)

MILES: Cut! Excuse me; we're filming here. If you absolutely must walk in front of our cameras, could you at least pretend to be zombies?

(DENISE rolls her eyes.)

MILES: Please, I may be a kid, but so were all the famous directors. We all have to start somewhere.

(ED, DANIELLE, SUMMER, BRAD, and DENISE exchange glances.)

MILES: Please, please, will anyone listen to me? I just need you not to walk in this little tiny area here while we film for, like, ten minutes. Just walk around us. Please! *(Beat.)* This is my fourth film. I am not an amateur! I demand respect!

(ED, DANIELLE, SUMMER, BRAD, and DENISE stand and stare at MILES.)

MILES: OK, OK. Just stand like that. We'll pretend you're zombies. Action!

TORI: N—

DANIELLE: What are you doing?

MILES: I'm ruined. Ruined! You people are killing me. I'm just a kid but I'm having a heart attack and my ulcer is bleeding! The next Tarantino is dying on the sidewalk because you clowns can't keep from walking on this tiny bit of sidewalk for five minutes. That's it! I quit! I can't take this anymore! Nothing works out for me! I hate everyone! I can't work under these . . . this . . . stuff! I quit!

(MILES takes his camera and storms off.)

ED: What's up with him?

Scene 2: Fuming

OLIVIA: Miles?

(Beat.)

KIM: Are you OK, Miles?

JUD: Let's film him.

TORI: Why?

JUD: It's a zombie movie, right? He looks like a zombie. Just keeps staring at us.

OLIVIA: Yeah. It's kinda creepy.

TORI: You should film *me*, not him. I was supposed to be the star of this movie. I really thought this was going to be great for me. My mom is going to be so mad; Miles is going to be in big trouble if he doesn't finish this. My mom has been taking me to acting lessons for two years now, and Miles promised this film was going to be great. He said I could definitely take this to agents and get some major work. And I trusted him! He told me he'd give me lots of close-ups and camera time! I'm perfect for film work. Look how cute I am! This kind of thing is not supposed to happen! I'm supposed to get this film done and then an agent is supposed to see it and then I'm supposed to get a job in a film with Tom Cruise and then I'm supposed to be famous forever and ever. It's not supposed to go like this. I'm supposed to be a star! A star!

KIM: I thought we were all the stars of this movie.

TORI: I was the *main* character! You were just zombies.

OLIVIA: Yeah, but it's a *zombie* movie. Not a *girl running* movie.

TORI: But it's about me escaping the zombies.

JUD: Wow. She's going nuts, too.

KIM: Don't fight, guys. We need to get Miles back. Miles? Can you hear me?

TORI: Can you believe that girl who tried to take over? She thought she was an actress.

JUD: She was good.

TORI: What?

JUD: I thought she was good.

TORI: She was not.

OLIVIA: She wasn't bad.

TORI: Yes, she was!

KIM: It doesn't matter anymore. There's no movie. Do you think Miles is stuck this way?

OLIVIA: He'll snap out of it.

JUD: Do you think we should stuff some food in his mouth or something?

KIM: He might choke.

JUD: Right. I'm just hungry, that's all.

(GIA and TRAVIS enter.)

GIA: Is he all right?

OLIVIA: He will be.

GIA: Because Travis and I really got the acting bug now and we want to be superstars already.

TRAVIS: Yeah. I want gold teeth.

GIA: Well, now you're talking crazy, Travis.

TRAVIS: I can do whatever I want with my superstar money, Gia.

GIA: Fine, but you're going to look stupid.

TRAVIS: I'm going to look cool.

GIA: Right. You wish.

TRAVIS: I will.

TORI: Well, Miles is not ready to start filming again, so I guess you'll just have to go home.

GIA: You are so jealous 'cause I was better than you.

TORI: Were not!

(ED, DANIELLE, SUMMER, BRAD, and DENISE enter.)

BRAD: So what's wrong with that guy? Is he just crazy?

GIA: He is a *director*, an *artist*. He's *sensitive*.

ED: I think he's crazy.

SUMMER: Why do his lips keep moving like that?

KIM: Don't know. Every once in a while he looks like he's going to talk, but no sound comes out.

DENISE: He's definitely crazy. Maybe we should take him to the hospital.

BRAD: How? We don't have a car.

OLIVIA: He's going to be OK.

TRAVIS: He's a zombie! He was doing a movie about zombies and now he's one himself. That is creepy.

GIA: You are so right, Travis! I am creeped out.

SUMMER: Do you think it's contagious?

ED: Zombie-ism?

SUMMER: Yeah.

ED: No way. Plus, he's not really a zombie. Nobody ate his brain.

DENISE: We blew his brains. He totally lost his brain. You saw him!

KIM: Miles? Miles!

(KIM shakes MILES. MILES snaps out of his trance a little.)

MILES: Action! Places! No! Get away! Places! Action! Lines! No!

DANIELLE: He's broken. Like one of those talking dolls, only broken.

MILES: Places!

DENISE: Let's get out of here before we get into trouble.

(ED, DANIELLE, SUMMER, BRAD, and DENISE exit. JUD starts filming.)

MILES: Rolling! Places!

JUD: This looks excellent.

KIM: Jud, you should really stop. He's sick. It's not nice.

JUD: It's a documentary now.

TRAVIS: Hey! I'll be a witness. Today at two P.M., I think, I saw this boy turn into a zombie. It was really . . . embarrassing. For him. He went completely bonkers. One minute he was a bossy film director—I was one of the starring actors—

TORI: No, you weren't! I was the star!

GIA: I don't think so!

JUD: Fight!

KIM: Don't, please!

TRAVIS: Let me re-create what happened. First, there were people walking in front of the camera while they were filming the movie. "Hi! I'm just walking along the street! I don't know what I'm doing!" Then there was this guy, the director. And he was like, "What are you doing? This is a film set! I can't take this anymore! Aaah!" Then he was a zombie, just like that. Went from completely angry to nothing. Just staring. So far he hasn't eaten any brains, but who knows? It could happen. In fact, I don't want it to happen to me. I want to be a superstar and make lots of money so I can get solid gold teeth and tattoos, but I do not want my brain eaten. Gia, let's get out of here. This guy is freaking me out. Let's go make our own movie or something.

GIA: Great idea! I bet we'd be great filmmakers. Then we can be the stars *and* the directors. We can do anything we want! I want to be a beautiful princess from France or someone who's in disguise—

TRAVIS: Can't you be a robot or something?

GIA: Well, OK. I'll be a beautiful robot—

MILES: Action!

GIA: See? This is good stuff! Let's go, Travis.

(TRAVIS and GIA exit.)

TORI: Good riddance. I knew she'd never make it. Look, my mom is going to be here to pick me up in an hour. Can we put together a documentary by then?

JUD: I guess so. I don't know how it works.

TORI: So put the camera on me.

(TORI takes a deep breath.)

TORI: Today, a tragedy occurred. This young man completely lost his mind. He was very talented and very young so this is very sad. *(Pretending to cry.)* I don't know if I can continue talking about it! But I will try. He's so brave! He had completed most of his film when this—this is so difficult!—when this tragedy occurred. Miles? Miles? Can you hear me? Come back to us! We need you! *(Long beat.)* Oh, God, why did you take such a young life! Miles had everything going for him. I don't know how I'll go on! The world has lost a—

MILES: Cut! Cut! Cut! Cut! CUT! That was terrible! No overacting. Now places, everyone, please! Let's get this done!

KIM: Miles? Are you OK?

MILES: I said, "Places!"

OLIVIA: I think that's a yes.

MILES: What are you doing with my camera?

JUD: I was making a documentary about the making of the movie.

MILES: The camera's not running.

TORI: You're kidding! And I was doing such good stuff!

MILES: Places. And no overacting. Do you know your lines? "No! Go away! No!"

TORI: Of course I know my lines.

MILES: Then let's go! Zombies, you're hungry. You're tired.

JUD: I really feel it now. I'm so there.

MILES: Then let's go! Action!

TALK BACK!

1. Describe a time when someone did not take you seriously. How did you react?

2. If you could do any job in the world, what would it be and why?

3. Who are you most like in this play?

4. Do you think you'd be a better actor or director? Why?

5. What makes a suspense or horror movie good or bad? What scares you?

6. If you were to make your own movie, what kind of film would it be (comedy, drama, romance, science fiction, etc.) and why?

7. Why do Tori, Gia, and Travis want to be stars so much? Do you feel the same way? What are star qualities?

BAD CUPID

3F, 4M

WHO

FEMALES	MALES
Allison	Connor
Destiny	Cupid
Paige	Eli
	Icky Mickey

WHERE School.

WHEN Present day.

🎭 Remember that until Allison bumps into him, Cupid is invisible. Make sure you don't look at him when he moves or speaks.

✐ Put a Greek or Roman god in an everyday, modern situation and see what happens. Examples: Poseidon goes on an ocean cruise; Athena is in a wildlife preserve; Apollo goes to the beach.

Scene 1: Falling In

CONNOR: I hate everyone! I hate you, and I hate you, and I hate you, and I hate you! Most of all, I hate you, Allison!

(CONNOR exits.)

ALLISON: Why is Connor always so mean to me? I like him. I think he's nice.

PAIGE: He's got issues, Allison.

DESTINY: He's just a weirdo.

ALLISON: I think he's sad. Maybe there's something we can do for him.

PAIGE: Don't bother.

DESTINY: Paige is right. He's a lost cause.

ALLISON: I guess so. We used to get along though. Last year. Sure, he said I had cooties sometimes, but we were friends.

DESTINY: You did have cooties, didn't you?

ALLISON: No! How could you say that, Destiny! I was walking in the woods and someone found one tiny bug, a mosquito or something, in my hair. Not cooties!

PAIGE: Oh. That's still pretty gross.

ALLISON: It's not like I could help it. It's not like I was dirty or something. I just took a walk in the woods.

DESTINY: Whatever you say.

PAIGE: The bell rang. We'd better go inside.

(ALLISON, DESTINY, and PAIGE exit. CUPID enters.)

CUPID: I think this is a job for me—Cupid! Connor is not allowed to hate everyone. Hate is such an ugly thing. If I could make the world a more beautiful place filled with love . . . well, I'd be so very happy. Who should Connor fall in love with? Maybe his teacher! Let's take a look at her. *(CUPID closes his eyes and concentrates.)* Ah! She's too old and warty! Those girls out here a minute ago . . . maybe one of them. Allison seemed to like Connor, said they used to be friends. But that's too obvious. Paige was uninterested in him, so she'd be more of a challenge . . . Ha! As if anyone could be stronger than me! I've been doing this for ages. Even if someone just brushed against one of my arrows, they'd be madly in love. I'm that powerful. So how about that Destiny? She thought Connor was a weirdo. And her name is Destiny—how sweet! Destiny it is. Fast forward to the end of school!

(A bunch of KIDS file past CUPID very quickly with books in tow. Last to come out are PAIGE, ALLISON, DESTINY, CONNOR, and ELI.)

CUPID: Now to get everyone in place!

(CUPID puts DESTINY and CONNOR back to back, then clears a space so he can have a clear shot at DESTINY's heart. The KIDS do not notice CUPID; he

is invisible to them. The following dialogue happens while CUPID is putting everyone in place.)

ELI: I hate everyone, too. Everyone stinks.

PAIGE: I can't believe we have to do another essay.

CONNOR: Especially girls. Seriously. They talk too much.

DESTINY: I'll do your essay if you do my math.

ELI: What's the point of girls? They're pointless.

ALLISON: But what will you do when there's a math test?

CONNOR: Except maybe moms.

DESTINY: I wasn't serious.

ELI: Yeah, but they nag, too. If I have to hear "clean your room" one more time . . .

ALLISON: I knew that.

(CUPID is getting ready to fire his arrow. CONNOR bumps into DESTINY.)

DESTINY: Excuse you!

CONNOR: Excuse you, cootie girl.

DESTINY: I'll have you know I never had cooties. Allison did!

(ALLISON crosses in front of DESTINY.)

ALLISON: No, I didn't!

(ELI *walks toward ALLISON.*)

ELI: All girls have cooties! It's been medically proven.

CUPID: Can't everyone stand still for a minute? Never mind. I can do this. I am a master archer.

(CUPID *lets an invisible arrow go while PAIGE steps in front of its path.*)

PAIGE: Eli Nicholson, you're a cree—

(PAIGE *gets hit with the arrow.*)

PAIGE: —creative guy.

ELI: Well, yeah. I love to draw. Everyone knows that.

PAIGE: Your drawings are great.

ELI: Well, duh.

CUPID: Ah! Wrong kid! But it's OK. Everyone needs more love. Even Eli Nicholson. Now, let's try Connor and Destiny again.

(CUPID *takes out another arrow to aim at DESTINY.*)

PAIGE: I'd love to see your drawing some time.

ELI: Well, I could show them to you. They're pretty awesome.

DESTINY: Paige, what's wrong with you? That's *Eli*! The rudest kid in school?

PAIGE: Right. Eli. Eli, you have such nice hair. I never noticed it before.

(DESTINY walks over to PAIGE and starts to shake her as ELI gets out a notebook of his drawings.)

DESTINY: Snap out of it!

(CONNOR takes ELI's notebook and walks into the path of CUPID's arrow.)

CONNOR: Wow! WOW! These drawings *are* awesome! I love them. I really, really love them!

ELI: Give me back my notebook! I want to show them to Paige.

CONNOR: No way. You're never getting them back! I love them.

CUPID: These kids are driving me crazy! Can't they ever stand still?

ELI: I know they're awesome, but I want them back, man. They're mine.

CONNOR: Not anymore. Finders, keepers.

PAIGE: Let me see them. I want to see what Eli did. Eli with the creativity and the nice hair.

ALLISON: What's going on? Everyone's acting really . . . different.

DESTINY: The word is weird! Everyone is acting weird! What's going on here?

(CUPID *finally hits DESTINY with an arrow. ICKY MICKEY comes onstage.* He's *the kind of kid who picks his nose, snorts, scratches, and talks to himself.*)

ICKY MICKEY: Hey, what's all the noise? I was trying to imagine what it's like to fly the Millennium Falcon and you interrupted me.

DESTINY: Icky Mickey, I'm so sorry. So, so sorry! Can you ever forgive me?

ICKY MICKEY: I don't know. I was getting to the good part. I was about to move to light speed.

DESTINY: Seriously? Light speed? That is so interesting!

(*ICKY MICKEY starts to pick his nose.*)

ICKY MICKEY: Of course it is. Space travel is fascinating.

DESTINY: Can I help you with that?

ICKY MICKEY: What?

DESTINY: That!

(*ALLISON grabs a hold of DESTINY.*)

ALLISON: No way am I letting you pick Icky Mickey's nose!

DESTINY: Let go of me! I love him!

ALLISON: What's going on? Can't anyone help me? Connor, help me!

CONNOR: These drawings are so awesome! I want to marry them.

PAIGE: I want to marry them more. You're so talented, Eli.

ELI: Gifted. My mom says I'm gifted.

DESTINY: Let go of me, Allison! Mickey needs help!

ALLISON: No, he doesn't! Stop! Everyone, stop!

(DESTINY, ICKY MICKEY, CONNOR, ELI, and PAIGE stop and listen to ALLISON.)

ALLISON: Enough! You're all acting nuts! What's wrong with you? Paige, you don't like Eli. You said once that he was the most annoying guy in school and totally full of himself—and he is! No offense, Eli, it's just the facts. Don't you remember? And Connor, you hate art. Ever since kindergarten you've made fart noises in art class. So you're not interested in Eli's drawings. And Destiny, what can I even say to you? You've gone the most crazy out of everyone. Icky Mickey? Listen to his name again: Icky Mickey. He picks his nose. He acts really weirdly . . . he says all the wrong things . . . he's *icky*. You can't like him. You can't! And I'm absolutely, positively sure you don't want to pick his nose. So everyone can stop acting totally different now! The world needs to go back to normal. And in the real world I'm friends with Paige and Destiny, Connor is friends with Eli, and Icky Mickey does his own thing. And maybe I like Connor just a little, tiny bit, only he doesn't like me. Or only sometimes. OK?

(Beat. No one moves or speaks. Then suddenly, all together, DESTINY, CONNOR, and PAIGE go back to being in love.)

CONNOR: This notebook is mine!

PAIGE: I need it! Eli needs it! He's a genius!

ELI: I am! Give it back, Connor!

DESTINY: Dear, sweet Icky Mickey, come to me!

(ICKY MICKEY runs away from DESTINY.)

ICKY MICKEY: I'm not used to this kind of attention!

ALLISON: I give up! I'm out of here!

(ALLISON goes to leave and bumps into CUPID.)

CUPID: Uh-oh.

Scene 2: Falling Out

DESTINY: You're gross. Why did I ever like you?

ICKY MICKEY: I don't know. Because you're irrational and scary?

DESTINY: Takes one to know one.

ICKY MICKEY: Very mature.

DESTINY: Nose picker!

CONNOR: I don't need this lousy notebook anymore. I've traced over your drawings so many times I can do better myself. I'm a better artist than you, Eli.

ELI: Impossible! Right, Paige?

PAIGE: Whatever you say.

ELI: See?

PAIGE: How come you never really listen to me?

ELI: Huh?

PAIGE: I just said that kind of sarcastically, and you didn't even notice.

ELI: What are you talking about?

DESTINY: I hate boys.

PAIGE: I think I do, too.

DESTINY: Why did we ever think otherwise?

PAIGE: I don't know.

DESTINY: If anyone ever says I even spoke to Icky Mickey, I will kill them.

PAIGE: Allison was right. We went crazy.

CONNOR: Girls are airheads.

DESTINY: Whatever! You just spent weeks tracing drawing of dragons. You're a loser.

CONNOR: I know you are, but what am I?

(CUPID enters with ALLISON right behind him.)

CUPID: What's happening? Why is everyone falling out of love?

ALLISON: I love love. What could be better in the whole world than love? It makes you feel warm and bubbly inside. I'm going to feel this way forever. You're so great, Cupid. I'm so glad I met you. I've never met anyone so great. I love how you understand love. How you want everyone to love love like you love love. It's, like, amazing. You're not afraid, my brave and wonderful Cupid. So many boys are afraid of girls and love, but not you. You're different. Perfect. You're all about love. And you understand me. I'm allowed to be a girl around you. Most boys, if you want to be around them, you have to do boy things—watch sports, play video games, listen to conversations about science fiction. They won't compromise. They won't ever do girl things.

Would it kill them to go to the mall? But you are different. We're going to get married someday. I know it. We're meant to be together. Let's go shopping, Cupid. I want to buy you a pretzel.

CUPID: Allison, I think I've ignored my duties too long. Plus, I'm not ready for marriage.

ALLISON: What are you saying, Cupid?

CUPID: I think maybe we need to break up.

ALLISON: Did I do something wrong?

CUPID: No. It's not you, it's me.

ALLISON: No, it was me! You hate me.

CUPID: No!

ALLISON: You like someone else!

CUPID: No! I think I just need to take a break from girls. I'm still very young, you know.

ALLISON: You're three thousand years old!

CUPID: Very young for my people.

ALLISON: I ignored our age difference because I thought we had a connection!

CUPID: Well, we did. But not anymore.

ALLISON: I hate you.

CUPID: Don't you think that's a bit extreme? Just a minute ago you were saying how much you love me.

ALLISON: I was lying. You're ugly.

CUPID: No, I'm not. I'm handsome.

ALLISON: Who told you that? Your mother?

CUPID: Well, yes.

ALLISON: Did she also tell you that you were smart, clever, funny, and interesting?

CUPID: Yes.

ALLISON: She lied! Now go away.

CUPID: But I need to fix what I did here.

ALLISON: They're already fixed. We're all better off without you.

CUPID: Don't say that, Allison. You just need to find the right guy.

ALLISON: No kidding! Maybe one who's not three thousand years old!

CUPID: Exactly.

ALLISON: Don't agree with me!

CUPID: Oh. This is confusing.

ALLISON: And I thought you understood women.

CUPID: You're a girl.

ALLISON: And you're an infant.

CUPID: I'm three thousand—

ALLISON: I never want to see you again!

(ALLISON walks away.)

CUPID: I feel terrible. Maybe I can make it up to her. She used to like Connor, right? Maybe I can make this work this time. I'll need to be very careful. Things really didn't go well last time.

(CUPID stands off to the side.)

PAIGE: Allison, are you OK?

ALLISON: I hate boys.

DESTINY: We do, too!

ELI: You really don't.

PAIGE: Yes, we do. Especially you.

ELI: This is confusing. I thought you liked me.

PAIGE: No.

ELI: OK. Wanna get pizza, Connor?

CONNOR: Sure.

CUPID: No! Wait, Connor!

(CONNOR and ELI exit.)

PAIGE: I've just discovered something very important. I hate doing what other people want to do. I want to do what I want and if other people don't like it, they can bite me. Also, I hate pictures of dragons and devils. They're ugly. I don't like ugly things. Conversations about whether King Kong could beat up Godzilla are only interesting for about five minutes. You know what I've learned most of all? People listen mostly to what they want to hear. Even me. I kept hearing that Eli was nice and liked me, when really he just liked me complimenting him all the time. And even when I wasn't complimenting him anymore, he still thought I was. We're all demented, aren't we? No one listens to anyone. Why do we even bother? Why don't we just live alone and watch movies? Living in dreams is so much better than real life. Things actually go right.

DESTINY: Yeah, but then we'd be lonely, right?

ALLISON: Is that so bad? At least we're not disappointed.

DESTINY: There's got to be something in between. Where you can be yourself and not be sad or alone.

PAIGE: I don't know what that could be.

DESTINY: Someday it'll be better. It has to get better.

(CONNOR enters.)

CONNOR: Hey, uh, Allison? Want to have pizza with us? The rest of you can come, too.

ALLISON: I don't know.

DESTINY: Go on.

ALLISON: But I'm sick of boys right now.

DESTINY: But you've liked him forever.

ALLISON: But I'm here with you guys, my best friends.

PAIGE: It's OK. We're not hungry.

ALLISON: Are you sure?

DESTINY: You bet.

ALLISON: Thanks, Destiny. And you too, Paige.

CONNOR: I hope you have some money.

(ALLISON and CONNOR leave.)

DESTINY: What does she see in him?

PAIGE: You liked Icky Mickey.

DESTINY: Shut up!

TALK BACK!

1. What makes people attracted to each other? Is it mutual interests? Chemistry? Good looks?

2. Have you ever liked someone (as a friend or as a crush), then later thought, "What was I thinking?" What changed your mind?

3. When do you think people should start dating?

4. Psychologists say girls mature faster than boys. Do you think this is true or false? Why?

5. In many ancient cultures, people thought gods controlled every aspect their lives from the weather to their love lives. If you could be an ancient god, what would you like to control?

6. Do you think you'll ever get married? Why or why not?

7. What do you think being in love is like?

8. Does being in love guarantee a good marriage? Is it better to marry for love or to have an arranged marriage?

SICK DAY

5F, 10M

WHO

FEMALES
Charlotte
Kiara
Officer Sabatini
Erica
McKenzie

MALES
Corey
Dalton
Dmitri
Frisco
José
Randy
Officer Jackson
Officer Bray
Officer O'Roarke
Wyatt

WHERE The streets of New York.

WHEN Present day.

🎭 Whenever you have to act out any emotion or condition (like an illness), see if you can recall how you actually behave under those circumstances. Everyone is different; good acting comes from being true to yourself. If you whine when you're sick or bite your lip when you concentrate, integrate those things into your character!

✍ One day I was feeling very sick walking to the drugstore in New York, and I looked for a garbage can (just in case I had to puke). The only one nearby had a domed top on it, just like the one in this story. Though I didn't get sick and get my head caught in it, I thought, "That's just the kind of thing that would happen to me!" Write a play about an unlucky thing that happened to you or that you think might happen to you.

36

Scene 1: Trashed

COREY: I don't feel so good.

KIARA: How come?

COREY: Don't know.

KIARA: Maybe it's something you ate.

COREY: Don't know.

KIARA: What kind of sick are you?

COREY: Dunno—sick-sick.

KIARA: Well, are you going to faint or barf or . . . well, you know. Which one of those?

COREY: I don't know. I don't want to do any of those things.

KIARA: Of course you don't want to. Nobody wants to be sick.

COREY: I want to *play* sick so I don't have to do my homework; I don't want to *be* sick.

KIARA: Well, yeah. I'm your sister. I get it.

COREY: So what am I supposed to do, Kiara?

KIARA: We need to go home. And don't barf on me or anything.

COREY: I don't think I can walk home.

KIARA: Could you get on the bus?

COREY: No! No way. I'd totally puke.

KIARA: Then we've got a problem.

COREY: Do you have any money? Maybe we could try a taxi.

KIARA: Of course I don't have money for a taxi. You're just going to have to walk.

COREY: **I think I'm dying.**

KIARA: Don't be such a baby, Corey.

COREY: **I can't help it. I feel terrible.**

KIARA: You're not going to die.

COREY: I feel like it.

KIARA: You're *not*. So just stop it.

(COREY groans.)

KIARA: Are you really gonna die?

COREY: I hope not! **Do you think I could die for real? I feel like it, but I'm just a kid! I'm not ready to die. I can't be like those kids on TV who are in hospitals and stuff and they're all brave and laughing even though they're really, really, *really* sick. I always thought maybe if I was really, really, *really* sick maybe I'd find a way to be like that, especially** when celebrities and news crews came to see me, but, Kiara, I just don't think I can! I'm going to be a terrible sick kid! I'm just not ready for it. Maybe you can never be ready, but I don't want to die. Not now. Not here! I'm in the middle of the street! I ought to at least be in bed—and Mom should be getting me tea and toast! I don't want to go like this, Kiara; I don't want to die!

KIARA: You really *are* sick. You're going squirrelly. What's that word? You're delusional.

COREY: What's that mean?

KIARA: You're thinking stuff that isn't true.

COREY: So I'm not dying?

KIARA: I doubt it.

COREY: But what if I am?

KIARA: You're not, stupid.

COREY: I'm telling Mom you called me stupid.

KIARA: You'll probably die before you get a chance.

COREY: Stop it, Kiara! This is serious. Do you want those to be your last words to me?

KIARA: Corey, you're fine. You're just acting totally insane, that's all.

COREY: Maybe it's a mental illness. Except—

KIARA: OK. Enough. You need to shut your mouth and calm down. You're going to be OK, Corey. It's probably something you ate. Worst-case scenario, you get really sick, barf up whatever you ate, and you'll feel OK. That's it. You're not dying. You're not mentally ill—much. At least not any more than any other little brother. You're just sick. So we need to get home so Mom can take care of you instead of me. What you need to concentrate on now is moving your feet, also known as walking, and not getting sick on the sidewalk. You can do it. Just concentrate. And if you do feel like you're gonna be sick, first of all, face away from me. Second of all, find a garbage can to be sick in. I think that's probably better than hitting the sidewalk or another person or doing it in your book bag. Got it? Just think about putting one foot in front of the other and not throwing up.

COREY: Thinking about it makes me think I'm going to do it.

KIARA: Fine! Then think about something else.

COREY: Like what?

KIARA: Like a TV show.

COREY: But there's so much action; it makes me feel sick.

KIARA: You know you're driving me crazy.

COREY: Maybe you're sick, too. Mentally sick.

KIARA: If I am, then you made me that way.

COREY: I'm going to tell Mom you said that.

KIARA: Go ahead.

COREY: You're supposed to take care of me, Kiara.

KIARA: I am!

COREY: You could be a little nicer.

KIARA: I'm trying.

COREY: Well, it doesn't seem like it.

KIARA: Come on, little baby. You can do it. Put your little bitty feet on the sidewalk and take little steps home. You can do it!

COREY: That's not what I meant. Seriously, Kiara, what if I'm *really* sick?

KIARA: Once and for all, you're not. And if you were, you'd just stay home until you're better.

COREY: I don't want to go to the doctors or the hospital.

KIARA: You won't have to.

COREY: But I have a basketball game tomorrow.

KIARA: You'll be fine. Just think about getting home.

COREY: I can't think. I feel all weird.

KIARA: Keep walking, Corey. Don't make too much out

of this or anything, but I'm going to take care of you. You're OK.

COREY: Kiara, I think . . . I think . . . I think . . .

KIARA: What do you think? Let it out!

(COREY runs to a garbage can to throw up. The garbage can has an arch over the opening like many New York City garbage cans. COREY gets his head through the opening and barfs.)

KIARA: This is so gross. Do you feel better now?

COREY: A little.

KIARA: Let's keep going. We need to get home.

(COREY tries to get his head out of the can. He can't. It's stuck.)

COREY: Kiara?

KIARA: Come on, Corey. Let's get home. Then Mom can take care of you.

COREY: Kiara?

KIARA: Are you going to be sick again?

COREY: I don't know, but—

KIARA: Come on, Corey.

COREY: But . . . I'm stuck.

KIARA: What?

COREY: I'm stuck. I can't get my head out.

KIARA: You got it in, so you have to be able to get it out.

COREY: Kiara, it really smells in here. It's making me feel sick all over again.

KIARA: Come on, Corey. Get your head out. Try. You can do it.

(COREY tries to get his head out. He fails.)

COREY: I can't. It won't fit. I feel like my head is going to pop off.

KIARA: Well, now what? What am I supposed to do?

COREY: Don't leave me, Kiara.

KIARA: Maybe I should run home and tell Mom.

COREY: You can't leave me here!

KIARA: Well, I have to tell someone! *(Beat.)* There's a fire-house nearby. Maybe they can help.

(KIARA exits.)

COREY: Don't leave, Kiara!

Scene 2: Untrashed

RANDY: What's going on here? You say your brother's stuck in a garbage can?

KIARA: That's right. See?

RANDY: Kid, we're going to help you. My name's Randy and I'm with the fire station on forty-eighth street.

COREY: Great!

RANDY: Now if you got your head in here, you must be able to get it out, too.

COREY: But I can't!

RANDY: OK.

KIARA: So now what?

RANDY: Hold on. I'm thinking.

(Beat as KIARA and COREY wait patiently for RANDY to think of a solution.)

RANDY: I know!

KIARA: I knew you would know!

RANDY: We'll butter him. Then he'll slide out.

COREY: Are these your usual methods?

RANDY: This has never happened before as far as I know.

You're the first kid to ever get his head caught in a trash can.

COREY: Great.

RANDY: Do you have any money?

KIARA: For what?

RANDY: For the butter.

KIARA: Well, no. I didn't know we'd need money.

RANDY: Maybe the grocer will help out. I'll ask him to donate some butter to the fire department. Be right back.

(RANDY exits.)

COREY: It really smells in here. I think I'm gonna be sick again.

KIARA: Stop it, Corey. You're grossing me out.

COREY: Do you think I'm enjoying this?

(DMITRI enters.)

DMITRI: What's going on here?

COREY: Nothing! There's nothing going on here.

KIARA: My stupid brother got his head caught in the trash can.

DMITRI: You're kidding!

COREY: Thanks a lot, sis.

DMITRI: Let me take a picture of this.

COREY: No! No! Stop him, Kiara, please!

(DMITRI takes COREY's picture with his camera phone.)

DMITRI: This is going to be great.

COREY: Thanks a lot, Kiara.

KIARA: What was I supposed to do?

DMITRI: How did you get your head in there anyway?

COREY: Just messing around.

KIARA: He barfed in it.

COREY: Kiara!

(DMITRI dials a number on the cell phone.)

DMITRI: You are not going to believe this, man. I had to call you since you don't have a picture phone. I cannot believe you still don't have a picture phone. Anyway, man, there's this kid who has his head caught in a trash can out on the street—you know, one of those ones with the arch on the top of it so you can't just throw stuff into it? I don't know why they're built like that. Maybe 'cause you need to be more careful throwing stuff out with them. Or maybe the police think you can't fit a bomb in one. But I bet you could. Oh, the kid puked in the can, too! How funny is that? *(Beat.)* Hey, how come you can't get your head out if you got it in there?

COREY: I don't know.

DMITRI: He doesn't know. *(Beat.)* Hey, how come you don't call the police or fire department?

KIARA: We did. They're getting butter.

DMITRI: Butter? Dude, the police are going to butter his head to try to slide it out! You've got to get out here now!

COREY: No! Don't come out here! It's boring.

(OFFICER JACKSON enters.)

OFFICER JACKSON: What's going on here? Are you a gang?

DMITRI: No, sir! Why would you think that?

OFFICER JACKSON: Why are you kids all hanging around on the street together? Get moving! Go home.

KIARA: We can't.

OFFICER JACKSON: Oh really? Are you arguing with me, young lady? I'm an officer of the law of the state of New York.

KIARA: I know.

OFFICER JACKSON: So it's not a good idea to wise talk me.

DMITRI: We're not doing anything.

OFFICER JACKSON: *(Suspiciously.)* Oh really?

DMITRI: Really. The kid's got his head caught in the tras can. By the way, why is there an arch at the top anyway? It makes it hard to throw stuff into it, and I bet you could still put a bomb in it.

OFFICER JACKSON: You know something about bombs, do you?

DMITRI: No. Just asking a question.

OFFICER JACKSON: Maybe I need to take you into the station for questioning. You seem like a troublemaker, son.

DMITRI: No way! I didn't do anything wrong! I stood on the *public* street and asked a question!

OFFICER JACKSON: Resisting arrest, are we?

(OFFICER BRAY enters.)

OFFICER BRAY: What's going on here?

OFFICER JACKSON: We have a gang and a kid with a bomb.

DMITRI: I don't have a bomb! Where do I have a bomb?

OFFICER JACKSON: He's resisting arrest.

OFFICER BRAY: I can see that. I'll call for backup.

(CHARLOTTE, ERIKA, and MCKENZIE enter.)

CHARLOTTE: What's going on here?

OFFICER BRAY: We need backup now! This gang is growing in size by the minute!

OFFICER JACKSON: It seems we've infiltrated their hangout.

OFFICER BRAY: Let's take cover.

(OFFICER JACKSON and OFFICER BRAY exit.)

ERIKA: What is he talking about?

KIARA: No idea.

MCKENZIE: Is his head caught in the trashcan?

(DALTON, FRISCO, and WYATT enter.)

DALTON: That was a weird picture. No way! It's true!

COREY: I wish I'd died before this happened.

KIARA: No, you don't.

FRISCO: Good going, Corey.

COREY: Thanks.

WYATT: I don't get why you can't get your head out if you got it in.

COREY: *(Yelling.)* I don't know, OK!

FRISCO: Does it echo in there when you scream?

COREY: Yeah. And it's really loud, too.

ERIKA: You can barely hear it out here.

(RANDY enters with JOSÉ.)

RANDY: This great citizen is going to help the fire department. This is José. Everything is going to be OK, people. We have the butter.

OFFICER JACKSON: Are you here to back us up? Because we requested other police officers.

RANDY: No, I'm here to help the boy with his head caught in the trash can.

WYATT: This is so funny.

CHARLOTTE: And weird!

RANDY: Everyone, step back. José and I are going to save this boy's life.

(ALL except RANDY and JOSÉ step back.)

RANDY: José and I have melted thousands of pounds of butter.

JOSÉ: Mister, it was only four sticks.

RANDY: José and I have melted four whole sticks of butter. We are going to apply them to the boy's neck so he can slide out and get free.

MCKENZIE: I just love firefighters!

RANDY: Stand back, people. We don't know what's going to happen here. Go ahead, José.

JOSÉ : OK.

(JOSÉ pours "butter" on COREY.)

FRISCO: Now what?

ERIKA: Now he gets free, silly. Weren't you listening?

RANDY: *(To KIARA.)* What's his name?

KIARA: Corey.

RANDY: Corey, are you OK?

COREY: Well, it's disgusting, but I'm OK.

RANDY: Great. See if you can slowly, carefully slip out now.

COREY: I'm trying. I'm afraid I'm going to rip my head off.

JOSE: Gently. Do it gently.

RANDY: You heard José. Do just as he says. He's a grocer. He knows about butter.

(COREY manages to get his head free.)

COREY: Oh God, I thought I was going to die in there!

KIARA: Let's go home.

COREY: I think I'm gonna be sick! *(COREY heads for the trash can again. With difficulty.)* No, I'm OK. I'm OK.

KIARA: This time, if you're sick, just barf on the sidewalk. Away from me.

COREY: Good idea.

DALTON: Let's get out of here.

FRISCO: That's it?

CHARLOTTE: Poor Corey. We hope you feel better.

COREY: *(To DMITRI.)* If you really feel sorry for me, you'll get rid of that picture.

DMITRI: Sorry, man. It was too funny.

KIARA: Come on, kid, let's go home.

COREY: Thanks, Randy. Thanks, José.

JOSÉ: No se.

RANDY: Another job well done by the New York Fire Department.

(KIARA, COREY, CHARLOTTE, ERIKA, MCKEN-ZIE, DMITRI, DALTON, WYATT, FRISCO, and RANDY exit. Beat. Suddenly, OFFICERS BRAY,

JACKSON, SABATINI, and O'ROARKE swarm on the scene—no one's there except JOSÉ, who's standing quietly to the side.)

OFFICER BRAY: Escaped!

OFFICER JACKSON: Outsmarted once again.

OFFICER BRAY: Better luck next time.

OFFICER JACKSON: What is that smell?

OFFICER BRAY: That, my friend, is the smell of crime. And wherever there is crime, we will be there. We may be late because we're waiting for backup, but we'll be there. We cannot be defeated. We will win this war against crime. No vicious gang of children will stop us. It makes me happy to know when I settle down each night that I am taking care of the world. I feel safer just knowing I'm out there every day fighting injustice. It's very satisfying. Sure, this job is dangerous and I get cold standing outside on the beat in wintertime and people sometimes say mean things to me, but I am doing something that has a real impact on the world. Plus, I get free coffee and doughnuts everywhere I go. What could be better? I'll tell you what—nothing! I will stamp out this stench of crime with the fragrance of justice, which smells like a thousand roses. I will not be stopped from my duty.

OFFICER SABATINI: That was beautiful.

OFFICER O'ROARKE: *(Indicating JOSÉ.)* Who's this guy?

OFFICER JACKSON: Ah-ha! Clearly the leader of the gang.

JOSÉ : Who me?

OFFICER JACKSON: Yes, you. You're coming with us.

OFFICER BRAY: Another job well done, boys.

TALK BACK!

1. Were you ever unjustly accused of a crime or treated like you were a delinquent for no reason? What was the situation? How did it make you feel?

2. Where would you go for help if you were in Kiara's situation?

3. When you're sick, how do you like to be treated?

4. Would you be sympathetic toward Corey like Charlotte or would you make fun of him like Dmitri? Why?

5. What do you think happens to José in the end? Why?

6. What would you do if you felt sick in public like Corey and were nowhere near a restroom?

7. Are you calm under pressure like Kiara or do you panic like Corey?

CRUSH

6F, 3M

WHO

FEMALES	MALES
Julie	Anthony
Meghan	Paul
Pru	Rob
Suz	
Sena	
Trina	

WHERE School

WHEN Scene 1: A school dance; Scene 2: The next day.

🎭 Keep the energy up throughout the scenes. Remember energy and speed are not the same thing. Go into the scene with a feeling of excitement!

✎ One time at a school dance I tried out a new dance move I thought was really cool. It wasn't. Write a scene about an embarrassing thing you did (or one from your imagination).

Scene 1: Squish

MEGHAN: I can't.

JULIE: Do it!

MEGHAN: I can't!

PRU: You'll regret it if you don't.

SUZ: Forever!

SENA: Come on, Meggie!

MEGHAN: I don't know . . .

SUZ: Yes, you do! You love him.

JULIE: You've loved him forever.

PRU: You'll regret it . . .

MEGHAN: Fine. I'll tell him. Now where is he?

SENA: I think he's by the bleachers.

MEGHAN: Where?

   (ANTHONY enters with TRINA.)

JULIE: Oh my God, I see him!

MEGHAN: I'm scared.

PRU: Don't be.

SUZ: You can do it.

MEGHAN: He's with Trina!

SENA: He's not *with* her. They're just standing together.

SUZ: It *does* kinda look like . . .

PRU: No way. They're not even talking to each other.

MEGHAN: That makes it even worse! They're definitely together then.

JULIE: No, really? Why do you think so?

MEGHAN: If they weren't together, they wouldn't stand right next to each other like that or they'd feel like they had to talk. But if they're standing together and not talking, then they *are* together. Get it?

JULIE: No. Not at all.

SUZ: I sort of get it.

MEGHAN: See? I'm doomed!

PRU: Whatever.

(JULIE, SUZ, SENA, PRU, and MEGHAN go silent. Focus shifts to ANTHONY and TRINA.)

TRINA: I wish I knew what to say to him. I mean, he's standing *right here*.

ANTHONY: This is, like . . . awkward. What should I say . . .

TRINA: Do I like him? I think I like him. Why won't he say anything? What am I doing here? I look like an idiot. I don't know what to do. Am I wearing the right thing? It feels good to be standing next to a guy. I wonder if people think we're together or not.

ANTHONY: *(Singing.)* Row, row, row your boat. Gently down the stream . . .

TRINA: What is he thinking? He looks deep in thought. Is he thinking he doesn't like me? Is he thinking of asking me to dance? I think I'm a good dancer, but what if I'm not? Or what if he's not? What if he's totally embarrassing, and I don't want to be seen with him anymore? What if he flails around like a dead fish? Or can't hear the beat. Or never asks me! Ask me, Anthony, ask me! *Ask me!*

ANTHONY: *(Singing.)* Merrily, merrily, merrily, merrily, life is but a dream.

TRINA: *ASK ME!*

ANTHONY: That's actually a pretty nice song. I never thought about the words before.

TRINA: He's so cute. Or I think he's cute. Is he cute or do I just think he's cute because other girls think he's cute?

ANTHONY: *(Singing. Getting into it.)* Row, row, row that boat. Row it!

TRINA: No, he's cute.

(Attention shifts from TRINA and ANTHONY back to SENA, SUZ, PRU, JULIE, and MEGHAN.)

SUZ: They're totally in love. I see it now. Meghan, I'm so sorry.

JULIE: No way! I think they hate each other.

SENA: I think they're just standing in the same place. I never heard anything about them being together.

PRU: We would've heard, right?

MEGHAN: Yes. Yes! We would've heard! Right?

JULIE: Not necessarily.

PRU: Why are we being negative?

JULIE: We shouldn't be negative. Anyway, you two are meant to be together.

MEGHAN: We are, aren't we?

PRU: Completely!

SUZ: Do it, Meghan!

SENA: You have to do it.

JULIE: Well, not *do it*. But do it.

SENA: Go for it.

SUZ: Go for it!

MEGHAN: Okay!

(Attention shifts to TRINA and ANTHONY as

MEGHAN gathers her courage and adjusts her clothes, etc. ROB and PAUL enter.)

ANTHONY: Hey! There are the guys.

TRINA: Oh yeah. *(To audience.)* That's the first thing he said to me all night practically!

ANTHONY: I'm gonna go talk to the guys.

TRINA: OK. Should I . . . I mean, do you want me to . . . go with you?

ANTHONY: No, no. You stay here. Relax. I'll . . . be back.

TRINA: OK. Great.

(ANTHONY walks over to ROB and PAUL.)

TRINA: *(Sarcastically.)* Real great.

MEGHAN: Oh my God! He went over to the guys! Now how am I going to talk to him?

PRU: What do you mean?

MEGHAN: They'll all be staring at me. The guys. If I go talk to him now. And he'll feel like he has to be really cool and laid back and not into me, know what I mean?

SUZ: I know what you mean.

JULIE: Could be embarrassing.

PRU: Can't you just ask him to step away?

MEGHAN: They'll still *know* and they'll get this big grin on their faces and Anthony'll see it and he'll act all cold and "I don't care" . . . See what I mean?

SENA: I see what you mean. Is there a way to get him away from them?

MEGHAN: You guys could go talk to those guys.

JULIE: Paul and Rob?

SENA: No way!

SUZ: I wouldn't know what to say.

JULIE: Paul kissed me in second grade. I wouldn't want to lead him on.

SENA: We should, though; it's a sacrifice for the sister-hood.

JULIE: I couldn't! I'm sorry, Meghan, but I couldn't!

SUZ: Me neither! It's too scary!

MEGHAN: So it's OK for me to do something scary, but not you?

PRU: But you *love* him.

MEGHAN: I don't *love* him.

SENA: You totally love him!

(SENA, SUZ, JULIE, PRU, and MEGHAN continue

to argue silently. TRINA fumes silently. Attention shifts to PAUL, ROB, and ANTHONY.)

PAUL: So, a dance. Dances suck. Why did we come?

ROB: Dunno. And Anthony here came with a girl!

ANTHONY: Yeah, well . . .

PAUL: Trina, though. She's nice. She's pretty cute, I guess.

ANTHONY: Yeah. Well . . .

ROB: Yeah, I guess so. Way to go, man!

ANTHONY: Thanks. She's OK.

PAUL: So what are you doing?

ANTHONY: Well . . .

ROB: Did ya make out or are ya saving that 'til later?

PAUL: Come on, man. Give it a rest.

ROB: It's a valid question.

ANTHONY: Well . . . Did you see the game?

ROB: Did I? We were robbed!

PAUL: Man, the game!

ANTHONY: The game!

(ROB, PAUL, and ANTHONY happily stand in

silence. MEGHAN, PRU, SUZ, SENA, and JULIE come over to them.)

SENA: Hey, guys, um, wanna dance?

PAUL: Uh . . .

ROB: Um . . .

(PRU, SUZ, JULIE, and SENA drag PAUL and ROB away.)

MEGHAN: So, Anthony, hi!

ANTHONY: Hi.

MEGHAN: So, I know this is weird and all, but I know you were looking at me in English class last week, so maybe this isn't weird, but even so there's something I have to tell you, and it's that I was thinking, well, I was wondering, well, I think but I want to know for sure, I mean, I could be wrong (it's been known to happen) but I just thought that maybe, since we get along so well, like you listen to me and understand me and we've known each other since kindergarten and this really isn't so weird because one time in first grade we pretended that we were married—remember that?—so this comparison is so normal and so not a big deal, but I was thinking . . . Do you like me? And do you want to go out sometimes? I mean, maybe you don't, and I would understand that. But I wanted to let you know that if you did, since you were looking at me, and all and my friends told me that maybe you did, that it would be OK with me.

(TRINA comes over to ANTHONY and MEGHAN.)

TRINA: Listen, Anthony, I just want to let you know that you're rude. Just an F.Y.I., but you're not supposed to leave your date standing *alone* for hours on end in the middle of the room. That's *rude*. And I don't like you anymore, just so you know. I think I like Joe, not you. In fact, I think I always liked him better than you and he looked at me in social studies, so he likes me back, too. So you're just going to have to be alone for the rest of your life. And I don't care if Meghan likes you because no one can really like you once they get to know how rude you are, Anthony. You're going to be one of those guys who sits on the couch watching TV and gets the remote lost in his butt crack and finds potato chips under the cushions and wears white socks with black shoes and pants that are too short. That's you, Anthony! You're that guy! So . . . Have a nice life!

(TRINA exits.)

MEGHAN: Whoa. Sorry. So. *(Beat.)* So? Anthony?

ANTHONY: Huh?

MEGHAN: So?

ANTHONY: So did you see Paul trying to dance? It's hilarious!

MEGHAN: So, Anthony? About us?

ANTHONY: Oh. Well, I . . . just don't think I'm ready for that kind of thing now.

MEGHAN: Oh.

(ANTHONY exits.)

MEGHAN: My. God.

Scene 2: Splat

MEGHAN: My life is over. It's over! Everyone knows. Everyone! For someone who never talks, Anthony has sure gotten the word around. I will never have a date in my entire life! Do you realize that? My whole life is over already. This is the saddest, most tragic day in my life! How could you let me make such a fool of myself? I really thought he liked me. One time in fourth grade he told me a joke! I mean, what am I supposed to think? And when we were pretending in first grade that we were married and that Jamie and Gail were our babies, he was way more into it than me. I kinda wanted Noah—do you remember him?—I kinda wanted him to be my husband instead of Anthony, but he was shy and didn't want to play. So I didn't even like Anthony at all, and that's why it's so cruel that he should be the one to ruin my social life forever!

PRU: Oh, Meggie, don't be sad. He's a dork. I don't even know why you liked him.

MEGHAN: I didn't!

SUZ: He's not even worth it. Forget about him.

MEGHAN: I will! I already have! But what about the rest of the school?

JULIE: They'll forget, too. Someone will kick someone in the groin or break their leg or whatever, and this'll all be over.

MEGHAN: Why did you push me into this?

JULIE: We didn't!

SUZ: We thought it was what you wanted!

SENA: He seemed nice at first.

PRU: Uh-oh. Trina's coming.

(TRINA enters.)

TRINA: So.

PRU: So.

TRINA: Well, you were trying to steal my boyfriend.

JULIE: He isn't your boyfriend.

TRINA: He was.

SENA: But he's not now.

TRINA: But she tried to steal him before he wasn't my boyfriend anymore.

MEGHAN: He looked at me in English, like, two weeks ago.

TRINA: He did not!

JULIE: He did, too. I can totally vouch.

TRINA: He was probably looking at me.

SUZ: I'm so sorry, Trina.

TRINA: Oh my God, he is such a jerk!

PRU: He's a total pig.

TRINA: Yeah! And to think that I liked him for, like, a week. And do you know that *he* asked *me* to the dance? People want to think it's the other way around, but it's not. It's was all him. I was surprised, too. I didn't think he liked me before that. He didn't show it. And now I find out that even while he was thinking of asking *me* to the dance, he was looking at *you* in English. Did he write you notes, too? And did he do that stupid snort when you said something funny? I thought that snort was cute for, like, ten seconds. Can you believe it? I am never going to be deceived again. I hate boys. They're stupid. He left me standing around at that dance for like *hours* while he talked to his friends. And everyone saw me standing alone. That is unacceptable. It is wrong. I hate Anthony Genoa. I hate him!

MEGHAN: Me, too.

(Beat.)

SUZ: He wrote you notes?

TRINA: Yeah. Really stupid ones.

JULIE: Did he ever write you a note, Meghan?

MEGHAN: Um, no. He just talked to me.

JULIE: Oh.

(Beat.)

TRINA: He never ever wrote you a note?

MEGHAN: No, OK? He just acted like he liked me, like, all of the time.

SENA: Yeah, but he never . . .

TRINA: Did he turn red and do that snorting laugh?

MEGHAN: Well, no. But we've known each other forever. We're totally comfortable together. That's why I thought we were supposed to be together.

PRU: Well, it could mean that. Or . . .

TRINA: Um, I have to go. I have to . . .

(TRINA exits.)

SUZ: It kinda does sound like he liked Trina more.

MEGHAN: But then why did he flirt with me?

PRU: Guys don't know what they're doing. Maybe he didn't even know he was doing it.

JULIE: Yeah. Or maybe he wasn't even flirting with you.

MEGHAN: He was!

SUZ: No, he was, Julie. Probably. He was flirting with her.

MEGHAN: I hate him.

SENA: We all hate him. He's dead to us.

MEGHAN: So what do I do now? I don't want to be "The Girl That Anthony Genoa Rejected" forever and ever!

SUZ: You won't be!

JULIE: Lots of guys like you.

MEGHAN: Like who?

JULIE: Like Paul, remember? He kept looking at Meghan while we were dancing. He was checking you out.

SUZ: Maybe . . . maybe he was looking at Anthony.

PRU: Anthony?! You think he's gay?

SUZ: No, no! I mean, because he was embarrassed to be dancing.

JULIE: No, he was looking at Meghan. I'm sure of it.

SENA: I think so, too. I mean, who would look at Anthony if they didn't have to?

SUZ: I guess so. You're probably right.

PRU: We are usually right. Just not about Anthony.

SENA: But the rest of the time . . .

JULIE: We're always right!

SUZ: What do you think about Paul, Meghan?

MEGHAN: I don't know. I never thought about him at all.

JULIE: He's not bad. In fact, I always liked his hair.

SUZ: Yeah! His hair.

MEGHAN: He can't really dance.

SUZ: That's true.

PRU: But who can? Hardly anybody. I mean Jamal can, but he's with Gina.

MEGHAN: Yeah, Jamal is off-limits.

JULIE: But Paul's not bad . . .

MEGHAN: He's a decent guy.

SENA: He loaned me a pencil once in math class.

SUZ: That is so sweet.

PRU: And so practical! That's a good thing, right?

JULIE: Definitely.

MEGHAN: His eyes are pretty nice, too.

SUZ: Yeah. Nice eyes, too.

PRU: What color are they?

SENA: Dunno.

PRU: What do you think, Meggie?

MEGHAN: Paul is pretty cute, I guess. You're sure he was looking at me?

SENA: Completely!

(TRINA enters.)

TRINA: Just so you know, Anthony and I are back together. He was just looking at you because you had a
spitball in your hair.

MEGHAN: Oh my God! I had a spitball in my hair!

TRINA: I guess so. So, bye.

(TRINA exits.)

SUZ: That was kinda mean of her.

JULIE: I think he was still *looking at you.* Know what I
mean?

SENA: Me, too. She's jealous.

PRU: Who needs her. Especially when you have Paul!

MEGHAN: Paul is so awesome. So much better than
stinky Anthony.

JULIE: You're so lucky to be in love, Meghan.

MEGHAN: I know!

TALK BACK!

1. Do you think Meghan's love problems are her fault or her friends'? Why?

2. Why do you think Meghan's friends encourage her to approach Anthony?

3. Why do you think Anthony asked Trina to the dance?

4. Do you think you're old enough to date or too young? Why? Do you think there's an age that's right for everyone or is it an individual decision?

5. Do you think dances are a good way for kids to socialize outside school? Can you think of any alternative ideas?

6. Do guys find it difficult to approach girls for a date? Why would it be hard?

LATER

3F, 1M

WHO

    FEMALES   MALES
      Hannah   Random Kid
      Katie
      Nicole

WHERE Outside somewhere.

WHEN Present day.

Think about your character's motivations: why he or she wants to do the things he or she does and what your character hopes to get from the other characters.

Rewrite Scene 2. What else could happen to Hannah?

Scene 1: The Lesson

HANNAH: What am I supposed to do?

KATIE: I don't know. Just talk.

HANNAH: And you're going to . . .

KATIE: Dunno. Just talk.

HANNAH: It's unseasonably warm.

KATIE: Why do you talk like that?

HANNAH: Like what?

KATIE: Like you're fifty.

HANNAH: Why do you say that?

KATIE: Like that!

HANNAH: What? I'm really not following.

KATIE: You did it again!

HANNAH: You really are quite nonsensical.

KATIE: You really don't get it?

HANNAH: You're going to have to give me an example.

KATIE: OK. What did you say about the weather?

HANNAH: I said it was unseasonably warm. It is.

KATIE: But a kid wouldn't say that.

HANNAH: Why not?

KATIE: It's not how kids talk.

HANNAH: That's not true.

KATIE: Sure it is. Nobody talks like that.

HANNAH: I do.

KATIE: That's just it! You're weird, Hannah.

HANNAH: Thank you very much!

KATIE: I'm trying to help. That's why kids don't like you so much.

HANNAH: That's not fair.

KATIE: Yeah, well, what do adults say all the time? Life isn't fair.

HANNAH: So, tell me then. What should I say about the weather?

KATIE: Well, you'd say something like, "Wow. It's warm. It's weird."

HANNAH: "Weird" means supernatural.

KATIE: What?

HANNAH: That's the meaning of weird. Like the weird sisters, the witches in Shakespeare's—

KATIE: Oh. Well. Whatever. Not anymore. Now it just means strange, odd.

HANNAH: Oh. Why?

KATIE: I don't know. Who cares? It just is. Why do you always need to know why? You must have been an annoying little kid, always asking questions. Why is the sky blue? Why—

HANNAH: Oh, I know the answer to that. The sky is blue because the sun hits particles in the air like dust or pollen. Light travels at certain frequencies, right?

KATIE: Never mind!

HANNAH: No, it's interesting. Why do people ask questions they don't want the answers to? Why do people not really want the answers to their questions when they're complicated and involve using your brain? Like all these diet miracle pills advertised on TV. They make your heart race, which makes you likely to have a heart attack, and if you're overweight, your heart is already working harder than a normal person's. So you're going to kill yourself. But it's much easier to take a pill than to exercise, so . . . I do understand the motivation, though; gym is my least favorite subject other than lunch.

KATIE: Everyone loves lunch!

HANNAH: I hate that awful feeling when everyone's sitting down, and you have to find a free spot. Once you find one you have to pray that no one says, "That spot is saved." Then you have to hope they don't talk to you or comment on what you're eating or want what you're eating. And since *I* don't like lunch, it's impossible for you to hypothesize that "everyone likes lunch"! It's simply untrue.

KATIE: This is going to be impossible. You'll never be a regular kid.

HANNAH: Sure I will. I'm smart. I learn fast. Let me try.

(RANDOM KID walks by in baggy pants.)

HANNAH: Look at that . . . *kid*. His navy slacks look to be several sizes too large. How . . . *weird*.

KATIE: *(Sighs.)* Close. His pants were big, they didn't "look to be several sizes too large." Kids don't say large. And they *don't* say slacks! Never, never, never slacks. And the color was blue, not navy. Never say navy as a color.

HANNAH: This is hard.

KATIE: Do you want to survive in this world or not?

HANNAH: Indubitably.

KATIE: Does that mean yes?

HANNAH: Yes.

KATIE: Say "yeah."

HANNAH: Yeah.

KATIE: Now I don't even remember what we were talking about.

HANNAH: You asked whether I want to survive in this world or not. Of course I do. I need to survive in this world. I have nowhere else to go. No one's yet colonized Mars or the moon.

KATIE: Right. Then you have to talk sloppy.

HANNAH: But it makes one's IQ sound low—

KATIE: Thanks! I talk like that.

HANNAH: Well, you ought to have said "sloppier." It sounds wrong.

KATIE: Hannah, *do you want to do this*—

HANNAH: Yes, yes, yes. Very well. I mean, yeah. What else do I need to learn?

KATIE: You need to wear better, more modern clothes. Like pants.

HANNAH: I like skirts.

KATIE: No one likes skirts. Not really. Not for all day. And if you wear a skirt, it needs to be short.

HANNAH: I don't think that's . . . right.

KATIE: It's right. You have to trust me.

HANNAH: I mean, I just don't know if I'd feel comfortable. I'd feel too . . .

KATIE: Naked?

HANNAH: I guess so.

KATIE: Sooo, wear pants!

HANNAH: Fine. But do they have to show my stomach so much? And pants show your . . . backside so much more.

KATIE: Butt.

HANNAH: But what?

KATIE: They show your butt.

HANNAH: Whatever you say.

KATIE: Say it.

HANNAH: No.

KATIE: Say it.

HANNAH: No, Katie. I don't want to.

KATIE: Say it!

HANNAH: But—

KATIE: That's better.

HANNAH: Maybe we should just forget it. I'll just be a— a—weirdo. It's OK.

KATIE: You said weirdo! I'm so proud of you! Now say dork.

HANNAH: Dork.

KATIE: Now say it to that kid.

(RANDOM KID crosses the stage again.)

HANNAH: Dork!

RANDOM KID: Drop dead, dweeb!

HANNAH: As though I would! I'm healthy!

KATIE: I think you mean "as if."

HANNAH: As—

KATIE: It's too late. He's gone. Give it a rest.

HANNAH: Why are you bothering with me anyway?

KATIE: I don't know. I guess since you're here, and I have to be seen with you.

HANNAH: I can go away if you want.

KATIE: Nah. I don't mind. You're not bad. Just weird.

HANNAH: I'm not weird! Maybe *you* are!

KATIE: You're learning so fast! It's good that you have a bad temper. That's going to keep kids from picking on you so much once we're done with your makeover. Oh, but one thing. Never, never, never get upset; you know, like crying? You can't ever let anyone see that they made you want to cry. So get angry. That's good. Even better is not caring at all.

If you can look like "whatever!" that's the best thing of all. Kids like to pick on the weaker kids because it's easy. And for some kids, it's fun. You know, the mean kids. And the best way not to be a target is not to care. Or to be a bully. Or to be the one making fun of other people.

HANNAH: That's not right.

KATIE: It's not right. It's wrong. It's cruel and terrible. But that's life, kiddo. Eat or be eaten.

HANNAH: Aren't there any other alternatives?

KATIE: Alternatives? Oh! You can also try flattery. There's a trick to that, too. If you're too needy, like you want the approval of the cool kids, that doesn't work. You have to not care. You can care later, when you go home.

HANNAH: Can't a person care about anything? Isn't that what makes us human?

KATIE: No, silly! What makes us human is the ability to talk and put on our own clothes!

HANNAH: Seems like you have to walk around like a zombie.

KATIE: It is a little like that sometimes. But only when someone's being mean. The rest of the time, with your friends and stuff, you can be normal. You just have to go zombie when things get weird. Actually, that's a funny thought. Next time someone says something obnoxious to me, I'll think, "I'm going to eat your brain!"

HANNAH: What?!

KATIE: Too weird?

HANNAH: You say that word a lot.

KATIE: There are worse words.

HANNAH: Yes. Like calling someone stupid. My mother always taught me not to say that.

KATIE: I have so, so, so much to teach you!

Scene 2: The Monster

HANNAH: I know! I was like, whatever. And she was like, uh! And I was like, um, whatever floats your boat.

NICOLE: Totally.

KATIE: Hannah, want to go to the mall?

HANNAH: As if! The mall is so yesterday.

NICOLE: Totally!

KATIE: OK. Well, can I hang out with you?

HANNAH: I guess.

(Beat.)

KATIE: So, what's going on?

HANNAH: Like, nothing. It's totally boring.

KATIE: Oh. Done any new science experiments lately?

HANNAH: As if!

NICOLE: Gross! As if!

KATIE: I created a monster.

HANNAH: In, like, a lab?

KATIE: No, I mean you.

HANNAH: Whatever!

NICOLE: I'm so sure! What is she talking about?

HANNAH: Color me clueless.

KATIE: Well, you used to be smart and kinda weird, and now you're—

HANNAH: Weird? No one says that anymore.

NICOLE: That is so funny.

KATIE: Not really.

HANNAH: Sure it is, dork!

KATIE: Zombie!

HANNAH: I know you are, but what am I?

KATIE: I'm not a zombie, you are.

HANNAH: So what if I am? Maybe you should watch out then.

KATIE: Are you gonna eat my brain or something?

HANNAH: Maybe I am.

NICOLE: *I'm* hungry.

KATIE: Quit it.

HANNAH: Let's get her.

KATIE: Stop it!

(NICOLE grabs KATIE. KATIE shakes free and runs to the other side of the stage.)

KATIE: This isn't funny.

HANNAH: Who's being funny?

(HANNAH and NICOLE slowly, mechanically walk toward KATIE.)

KATIE: Stop!

(HANNAH and NICOLE keep coming. When they reach KATIE, she dodges them and crosses to the opposite side of the stage. HANNAH and NICOLE slowly turn around and advance toward KATIE again.)

KATIE: Seriously, this is not funny!

HANNAH: It's hilarious!

NICOLE: I'm so hungry!

(This time, NICOLE and HANNAH catch KATIE.)

KATIE: Why are you doing this?

(HANNAH stops for a moment. NICOLE is about to take a bite out of KATIE's brain.)

HANNAH: Hold on, Nicole.

NICOLE: Do I have to?

HANNAH: Totally.

(NICOLE whines as HANNAH thinks.)

HANNAH: Why are we about to eat your brain? Hmmm. Well, it's a survival of the fittest thing, I guess. If we don't eat your brain, then we'll get weak. Then we're dead. But you'll be fine, Katie! You don't want your brain anyway. It doesn't help. It's better not to have one. You don't have to think or feel anything. Think of how strong that makes you. No one can hurt you because you can't think about what they've said or done. You don't have to say or do anything clever, you just say and do what everybody else does. You just go with the crowd. It's fun. The zombie life is good. Everyone's got the same goal—to find the weak people and eat their brains. It's very satisfying. I used to worry and think, worry and think all the time. It was boring. I was sad. Now things are good! I have a friend— right, friend?

NICOLE: Right, friend!

HANNAH: And no one bothers me or picks on me anymore. This is all for the best, Katie. You'll thank me later.

(HANNAH is about to bite into KATIE's brain.)

KATIE: See? See? The real Hannah is still in there!

HANNAH: No, she's not.

KATIE: Yes, she is! All that talk about being a zombie was intelligent!

HANNAH: No, it wasn't. Just zombie-talk.

KATIE: No! No, it wasn't. Did you understand it, Nicole?

NICOLE: Totally.

HANNAH: Ha! So there!

KATIE: Nicole, why is the sky blue?

NICOLE: Totally.

KATIE: That's practically all she can say! She wasn't responding to you.

HANNAH: No way. You're lying. Nicole, is my outfit cute?

NICOLE: Totally!

HANNAH: See? She's fine!

KATIE: Hannah, why is the sky blue?

HANNAH: Like, who cares?

KATIE: You do!

HANNAH: As if.

KATIE: Light bounces off crud in the atmosphere or something.

(HANNAH sighs.)

HANNAH: You can't un-zombie someone. So stop trying. It's not going to work.

KATIE: It's working already.

HANNAH: Categorically, absolutely untrue.

KATIE: Ah-ha!

HANNAH: Nooo! I was happy!

KATIE: You weren't happy!

HANNAH: Yes, I was!

KATIE: No, you weren't.

HANNAH: So why did you change me into a zombie in the first place if you didn't want me to be happier?

KATIE: It's not that I wanted you to turn into a zombie yourself, Hannah. I just didn't want you to be zombie food. You were too weak. They were going to tear you apart until you didn't exist. So I wanted to help. But I still wanted you to be yourself! Maybe I took it too far. Maybe you *should* say "indubitably" and all that stuff you said before. I bet that's what rich people say. I bet you'll be rich and successful when you're older, way more than the zombies, because you're smart.

HANNAH: That's what my parents say.

KATIE: Sometimes parents are right when they say stuff like that. I hope no one over thirty heard me say that! So, maybe you just need to get through the next ten years or so. Just survive them. That's all I was trying to do. Give you some survival skills.

I didn't want to change you completely. Can you understand that? And can you forgive me? And can you go back to being your regular, un-zombiefied self?

HANNAH: Of course I understand. I am highly intelligent, for a zombie. Maybe there's still some of my brain left. I suppose I forgive you. But can I go back to being my old self? I don't think so. I think I'll eat your brain. Let's get her, Nicole.

KATIE: Nooo!

(NICOLE and HANNAH pull KATIE to the ground and eat her brain. When they're done, NICOLE and HANNAH stand.)

HANNAH: How do you feel?

NICOLE: Totally!

HANNAH: No, not you.

NICOLE: Oh.

(KATIE stands.)

KATIE: I feel . . . OK. I feel . . . blank.

HANNAH: It's great, isn't it? You're totally carefree.

NICOLE: Totally!

HANNAH: Shut up.

NICOLE: Oh.

KATIE: I guess, but . . . I miss something.

HANNAH: No, you don't.

KATIE: I think I do.

HANNAH: No, you don't.

KATIE: I guess I don't.

HANNAH: See?

KATIE: How will I pass my classes now?

HANNAH: Just smile.

KATIE: What about my parents? Won't they notice?

HANNAH: They'll be happy at how nice you are now.

KATIE: Oh. Isn't it uncool to get along with your parents?

HANNAH: Well, just tell your friends your parents stink.

KATIE: Oh. Will my flesh start rotting?

HANNAH: It's cool. Everyone's flesh is doing it.

KATIE: Oh. Excellent.

HANNAH: Totally.

KATIE: Totally.

(Beat.)

HANNAH: You can say it now, Nicole.

NICOLE: Totally!

TALK BACK!

1. Do you think everyone tries to act the same?

2. Is it positive or negative to try to fit in and be like others? Explain your answer.

3. Do you feel pressure to fit in?

4. Did Hannah go too far?

5. What are the benefits of being smart and nerdy?

6. Are there any negative things about being popular?

7. What additional tips might you give Hannah in Scene 1 to help her be more cool?

WITCHCRAFT

2F, 3M

WHO

FEMALES   MALES
  Daisy   Antonio
  Lara   Jake
                   Lucas

WHERE   Outside, on the way to school.

WHEN   Before school.

🎭   Make sure you see the magic happening offstage in your imagination. If you see it, the audience will too.

✎   You have magical powers for one hour. What do you do? Write a play about it.

Scene 1: The Bully, Part 1

LARA: I don't want to go to school.

LUCAS: Who does?

DAISY: No one.

ANTONIO: School is not fun. Sure, every once in a while you get pizza day or tater tots, but when a tater tot is the best part of your day, it's not such a good day, is it?

LARA: No.

LUCAS: All you ever think about is food.

ANTONIO: I like food.

LUCAS: Everybody likes food.

DAISY: I don't like tater tots.

ANTONIO: What? Are you nuts? They're the only things to keep me going during the day, practically. The hope that I'll get tater tots later on is all that gets me through.

LARA: You need help.

ANTONIO: No, seriously!

LUCAS: Exactly. Seriously, you need help.

(JAKE enters.)

JAKE: OK, give me your lunches.
DAISY: What?

JAKE: GIVE. ME. YOUR. LUNCHES.

ANTONIO: This is my worst nightmare.

LARA: Why should we?

LUCAS: Don't argue, Lara. Just do it.

(LUCAS hands over his lunch.)

LARA: I don't want to. I want my lunch.

(JAKE walks up to LARA.)

JAKE: Give me your lunch.

LARA: What are you going to do, hit me?

JAKE: Yeah.

LARA: You'd hit me? A girl?

DAISY: We'll tell.

JAKE: Who are you gonna tell?

DAISY: The principal.

JAKE: That would only make things worse.

LUCAS: He's not kidding.

LARA: Why?

JAKE: Because I will take your lunch for the whole year,

whether I want it or not. Because I will make your life very unpleasant.

DAISY: What are you getting out of this?

LUCAS: Don't do the Dr. Phil stuff, Daisy.

JAKE: Well, *Daisy*, I am getting your lunch out of this.

DAISY: Yeah, but no one likes you. You have no friends. You only have lunches. You like that?

JAKE: Yeah, I like that, *Daisy*.

DAISY: Why do you keep saying my name like that?

JAKE: Because your name is stupid, *Daisy*.

DAISY: I have a nice name, *Jake*.

JAKE: Are you giving *me* attitude?

DAISY: I—I guess I am.

LUCAS: Daisy, stop. Listen, Jake, she didn't mean it. She doesn't know. Daisy, just give him your lunch and let's get to school. He *will* hit you. I've seen him do it.

DAISY: That's terrible!

LUCAS: Yes, it is. But that's how it is. Who knows why? But right now, let's not wonder. Let's get to school on time.

DAISY: But if you hit me, I'll have a mark on me. You'll get in trouble.

JAKE: Man, you're dumb. First of all, I don't care if I get into trouble. Second of all, maybe I'll twist your arm 'til you cry instead. I don't know. I have a lot of moves. There are lots of things I could do. Push you. Pull your hair. Knock you to the ground. Punch you in the gut . . . There's a whole world of moves I could do. People think bullying is so simple. Well, it's not. It's an art. You have to know what you're doing. It's not that easy getting everyone scared of you. Sure I'm big and that helps, but you know that there's lots of big kids who aren't bullies. They don't have it in them. You've either got it or you don't. And I've got it. So it would be stupid not to take advantage of it. And what I "get" from all of this is fear, respect, lunches, money—anything I want. Do *you* get anything *you* want?

LARA: I do.

ANTONIO: She does. Her parents are really nice.

JAKE: You.

ANTONIO: Who, me?

JAKE: You. You've been quiet all this time.

ANTONIO: Uh, just showing you some respect.

JAKE: Why don't you show me your lunch?

ANTONIO: I, uh, don't have a lunch.

JAKE: You don't have a lunch.

LARA: Oh. I see now, Daisy. He's hard of hearing. That's why he's so mean.

DAISY: *(Loudly.)* You don't have to be mean just because you're deaf!

JAKE: I'm not deaf! I was just repeating what he said. So shut up before you *really* make me mad!

DAISY: *(To LARA.)* He's not deaf.

LARA: I know. I heard.

JAKE: *(To ANTONIO.)* Lunch. Now.

ANTONIO: I don't have a lunch.

LARA: Oh, he's got no memory! That's why he's mean. I can see why that might make you mean. It must seem like no one ever listens to you, right? That is so sad. What is it like to have no memory? Do you put food in your mouth, then wonder how it got there? Oh my God! That's why you steal so many lunches! You forget you've already had lunch, so you keep eating lunch all day. That's so weird! I bet you get in trouble a lot at home, too. Your mom is probably like, "Jake, go clean your room!" And you say, because everyone says, "In a minute, Mom!" Then in a minute you totally forget you were supposed to clean your room, so then your mom gets all like, "Jake, I told you to clean your room, so clean your room now, mister!" And you're like, "What? What are you talking about? Why are you always mad at me?" It must be so hard. No wonder you're a bully. Here, have my lunch, you poor thing.

JAKE: You're so stupid.

LARA: See? He already forgot how smart I was just a second ago. Poor Jake.

LUCAS: No, Lara, he's just mean. It's just how he is.

JAKE: I am missing two lunches here. So hand them over *now.*

(DAISY thinks for a second, then hands over her lunch.)

DAISY: I think you're a creep and you're never get married and you'll always be alone.

JAKE: Good, 'cause I hate people. Especially girls. Especially you.

(DAISY opens her mouth to talk. LUCAS puts his hand over her mouth.)

LUCAS: Daisy, don't.

JAKE: That makes me one lunch short.

(JAKE walks up to ANTONIO.)

ANTONIO: *(In a high, tiny voice.)* I don't have a lunch.

JAKE: Even better. That means you have money.

ANTONIO: I don't have money.

JAKE: So you were going to starve.

ANTONIO: Yup.

JAKE: I am going to shake you upside down and see what's in your pockets.

(*JAKE pushes ANTONIO to the ground. ANTONIO quickly stands up again.*)

ANTONIO: No.

JAKE: What did you say?

LUCAS: Antonio . . .

ANTONIO: No! You can't have my lunch money. I love lunch!

JAKE: You are going to give me that lunch money one way or another . . .

(*JAKE chases after ANTONIO. ANTONIO runs offstage, followed by JAKE. ANTONIO runs back onstage and puts his hands out in front of him.*)

ANTONIO: NOOOOOO!!!

(*ANTONIO, LUCAS, LARA, and DAISY all stare offstage in JAKE's direction.*)

LARA: Oh.

DAISY: Wow.

LUCAS: No way.

Scene 2: The Bully, Part 2

LARA: Look what you did, Antonio!

DAISY: You are gonna be in sooo much trouble!

LUCAS: Maybe we should go to school now.

LARA: And leave him like this?

LUCAS: What else are we supposed to do?

LARA: But he's a person, too. True, he's a mean, terrible, nasty person, but he's still a person.

DAISY: He doesn't seem quite like a person, though.

LUCAS: Do you think you can change him back?

ANTONIO: I—I don't know.

LARA: You guys, this is just sinking in. Do you realize . . . Antonio did magic?

DAISY: It's not really possible, is it?

LARA: Well, there's the proof.

DAISY: But there wasn't a wand or magic words or an assistant in a little costume or anything.

LARA: Well, that just goes to show that we don't know how magic really works.

LUCAS: Yeah, but Antonio? Magic? Do something else.

ANTONIO: I don't wanna.

LUCAS: Scared?

ANTONIO: Yeah! What do you think? Do you want me to try doing something to you?

LUCAS: No!

ANTONIO: See? You're scared of it, too. I mean, this is a little cool, but it's also . . . weird.

LUCAS: Here's what I was thinking. Maybe you could change him back while we're at a safe distance. So if he comes after us, we'll have a head start. Then again, if you change him back, maybe *he'll* be scared of *you*. So then we won't ever have to worry about bullies again! You'll just give him the eye and wave your hands around a little and no one will ever say so much as an insulting word to us ever again. It might be fun to bully the bully. You could really torture him! Turn him into a spider then threaten to step on him. Or make him a hamster and force him to run in circles all day. He could use a little running. It seems like we're the ones always running, and he's just standing still, waiting for us to get tired. This could be fun. Maybe we could take him to school and show him to everyone. They won't believe it! Then he'll get a taste of his own medicine. Who looks stupid now, Jake? Who's a tiny, little wimp now, Jake? You are! Antonio, do you think this spell will last? If not, I'm pretty sure Jake is gonna kill me.

LARA: Has this ever happened before?

ANTONIO: Magic? No.

LARA: Well, listen; I think we need to be careful. Lucas, what you're saying would make us just the same as Jake. We'd be the horrible bullies, and I don't think that's right either.

DAISY: He is *really mean*, though.

LARA: Doesn't matter. It's not right. But I do think that maybe Jake won't bother us anymore. I think he's learned his lesson.

LUCAS: He's too stupid to learn a lesson. Aren't you?

DAISY: If he turns back, you are so dead.

LUCAS: I know.

ANTONIO: I think I'd better try to switch him back. Stand back, everybody.

(LUCAS, LARA, and DAISY step back. ANTONIO holds his hands up in front of him, closes his eyes, and waves his hands forcefully in JAKE's direction. JAKE reenters. ANTONIO, DAISY, LARA, and LUCAS stare at him. No one speaks for a beat.)

ANTONIO: So, anyway, you can't have my lunch money. I like lunch.

JAKE: I can't believe you did that to me.

LUCAS: How did you like wearing that girls' ballet outfit, Jake?

JAKE: You'd better shut up. I heard what you said.

LUCAS: Or you'll do what? Antonio here is my friend. I don't think you should make him mad.

JAKE: Then you'd better never, ever, *ever* go anywhere without him.

LUCAS: Antonio, change him back.

ANTONIO: No! I mean, not now.

JAKE: Listen, I won't bother you. I—I just want to go now.

ANTONIO: O—OK. For now.

JAKE: OK. Thanks. I, uh, gotta go.

DAISY: Wait!

(JAKE turns around slowly.)

JAKE: Y-yes?

DAISY: Our lunches?

JAKE: Here. Take them. I wasn't really hungry anyway.

(JAKE drops the lunches and exits in a hurry.)

LARA: You're magic, Antonio. You need to think about what you want to do with that.

LUCAS: Jake is scared of you! This is great!

LARA: You need to be responsible. It could be really dangerous to walk around turning people into half-mouse, half-lizard creatures. You could get in trouble. Go to jail or something.

LUCAS: But he could turn himself into something small and get out!

DAISY: Or, even better, he could melt the bars of the jail or something.

LUCAS: You're invincible!

LARA: Don't listen to them. Antonio, you have to be good. You have to do good things with your magic. You could help the poor and the sick—

ANTONIO: I could have any lunch I want! I could have fried chicken and French fries, chocolate chip cookies and ice cream, spaghetti and meatballs, a gallon of soda! This is the greatest thing that ever happened to me. I don't ever have to worry about getting fat—I can just magic myself thin! My mom would be so happy if I did that for her. She's always on a diet. And she hates carrot sticks. I could be rich, too, right? People would pay me a lot to make them thin. Plus, I could magic up money, right? You know, I don't get stuff like Harry Potter at all. How come they don't do magic to get them stuff like that? Christmas wouldn't matter anymore because every day would be like Christmas! I could get up and think, "What do I want today?" And when I don't want some of my stuff anymore, I can just magic it away or give it away to poor kids who aren't magic or I could just magic up a bigger house so there would be room for all my stuff. I'm the luckiest boy in the world! No one's ever going to bully me and everyone's going to like me for the rest of my life.

LARA: But if every day is like Christmas, Antonio, won't you miss Christmas? Won't it start seeming boring?

ANTONIO: It won't be boring ever.

DAISY: It might be. You might be able to have too much stuff.

LARA: And you might end up alone because you're so selfish.

ANTONIO: I'd share my stuff!

LARA: You'd have friends who only liked you for your stuff and your money.

ANTONIO: You say that like it's a bad thing.

LARA: It *is* a bad thing.

DAISY: It's like the kids being nice to Jake's face because they're scared of him. People would be nice to you only to get what they wanted from you.

ANTONIO: Well, you guys wouldn't, right?

LARA: No, but maybe I wouldn't like you at all. Maybe you'd be obnoxious.

DAISY: Maybe we couldn't even see you anyway because there would be so many other people around trying to get stuff from you.

LUCAS: I'd really like a BMX bike.

(*ANTONIO prepares to do some magic.*)

LARA: No, Antonio! Think about it first!

LUCAS: Oh, come on. Do it, Antonio. We're best friends.

ANTONIO: What did you bring for lunch?

LUCAS: Ham and cheese sandwich, juice, a cupcake.

ANTONIO: Sounds good. Give it to me.

LUCAS: You'll give me a bike?

ANTONIO: Give me your lunch, and I'll think about it.

LARA: So now you're exactly the same as Jake.

ANTONIO: Am not!

DAISY: Are too.

ANTONIO: I could turn you into goats, you know.

DAISY: See? You're a bully now, Antonio.

ANTONIO: I was going to do something nice in exchange for his lunch.

LARA: You threatened us!

DAISY: Let's get out of here.

(*LARA and DAISY exit.*)

ANTONIO: Girls! This is completely different than the Jake thing!

LUCAS: So where's my bike?

ANTONIO: Shut up or I'll put your underwear outside your clothes.

LUCAS: Look, I better hurry. If I'm late to school . . . Bye.

(LUCAS leaves.)

ANTONIO: What about giving me your lunch? I was totally gonna give you the bike! Lucas? *(Beat.)* I don't need you guys! You're going to be sorry! *(ANTONIO waves his hands around.)* See? Now you're all elephants. Ha ha. Should have listened to me. Should've been nicer to me, you guys. *(Beat.)* You guys? What are you . . . Don't guys. Seriously. I was kidding. Let's talk about this. Guys—

(ANTONIO runs off the stage in a panic as if elephants are about to attack him.)

TALK BACK!

1. Is power a dangerous thing? Why?

2. What would you do if you had magical powers?

3. Is Lara right about having too much being boring? Can you have too much stuff?

4. Why do you think people become bullies?

5. What do you think about Antonio's behavior at the end of the play?

6. If Jake confronted you, what would you do?

7. What material possessions would you fight for? Why?

LIZARD BOOTY

3F, 4M

WHO

FEMALES	MALES
Emma	Cameron
Lindsey	Harvey (the lizard)
Rachel	Jarvis
	Lars

WHERE Scene 1: Outside; Scene 2: A cave.

WHEN Present day.

🎭 Whenever possible, make what you do realistic. If you're supposed to have run a long way before entering, try running in place for a while before coming onstage. It will be much more believable than just pretending.

✎ I pulled two random words out of hat and used those words as my title; do the same. Make the words as odd as possible. It forces you to be creative!

Scene 1: Dreams

JARVIS: Race you.

CAMERON: Where?

JARVIS: There.

CAMERON: OK.

(JARVIS runs.)

CAMERON: You didn't say to go!

LARS: He's always running somewhere.

CAMERON: He says he wants to be prepared in case a wild animal chases him.

LARS: Why would a wild animal chase him? We live in the suburbs.

CAMERON: He had a dream once that a bear was chasing him.

LARS: I had a dream once that a doughnut was chasing me. You don't see me running.

CAMERON: Yeah, but you could eat a doughnut.

LARS: You could eat a bear, too.

CAMERON: But it's not as easy.

LARS: True. A good soaking in milk could waste a doughnut.

CAMERON: Why are we talking about this?

LARS: I forget.

(*JARVIS runs back in.*)

JARVIS: Beat you!

CAMERON: You didn't say when to start.

JARVIS: Now!

(*JARVIS runs off again.*)

CAMERON: One time I dreamed that my sister turned into a cockroach.

LARS: My sister *is* a cockroach. It's, like, a scientific fact. She even *looks* like a cockroach.

CAMERON: One time I saw this movie and this woman could turn her head all the way around. I tried to do it for a week. It sort of hurt. I wouldn't try it.

LARS: One time I tried to make my one eyebrow go up by itself like I was a villain in a movie for, like, ages.

CAMERON: So, can you do it?

LARS: I wish.

CAMERON: I can spit out food over a long distance. I used to do it all the time when I was little. If I didn't like something, I mean. My mother still won't give me brussel sprouts without covering her face.

LARS: I wish I were talented like that. I can only play the piano.

CAMERON: The piano's OK.

LARS: I like the drums. My mom and dad won't let me have them.

(JARVIS runs back in.)

JARVIS: Did you win?

CAMERON: Oh, no. I forgot.

JARVIS: So I won again!

CAMERON: I guess so.

JARVIS: Lars, want to race?

LARS: No, you'd beat me.

JARVIS: How do you know?

LARS: I can tell. You're faster.

JARVIS: I am fast. I'm faster than a bear.

LARS: That must have been some dream.

JARVIS: *(To CAMERON.)* You told him?

CAMERON: He dreamed a doughnut chased him. So now you're even.

JARVIS: A doughnut?

LARS: It was chocolate glazed.

JARVIS: Oh. *(Beat.)* Why didn't you eat it?

LARS: Woke up. Plus I was afraid it would run over me.

JARVIS: Just like my bear thing! Except bears don't get mushy in milk.

LARS: Yeah.

(EMMA, LINDSEY, and RACHEL jog onstage.)

JARVIS: What are they doing?

CAMERON: They're trying to be healthy.

LARS: Weird.

JARVIS: Lindsey!

LINDSEY: Yeah?

JARVIS: Did you have a dream?

LINDSEY: What?

JARVIS: A dream! Of being chased.

LINDSEY: What are you talking about?

(LINDSEY, EMMA, and RACHEL walk over to LARS, CAMERON, and JARVIS.)

CAMERON: I think they didn't have a dream.

LARS: So you're running to be healthy?

RACHEL: I've been running with my dad in the morning for a while now.

EMMA: It seemed like a good idea, so now we all do it.

JARVIS: So you didn't have a dream?

CAMERON: Give it up, Jarvis. There was no dream.

EMMA: A dream about what?

CAMERON: Being chased.

JARVIS: By a bear.

LARS: Or a pastry.

LINDSEY: You guys are nuts.

LARS: How come your dad jogs, Rachel?

RACHEL: My dad had a heart attack a few years ago. But he was really young to have one. So now we all jog to keep our hearts healthy. Plus, I think it's fun. It makes me feel really free, like I could do anything. It's really nice to have a family thing that we do together, too. And we don't really talk. So it's a family thing without all the questions about what you did and what you're doing and who your friends are and how you did on your test—all the stuff I hate to talk about. We just run. Sometimes we'll say, "Look out for that tree root," but that's about it. You should try it. We just did a mile. And now we're going to the old caves. That's about another two miles. You should come. It's very healthy. I used to have a hard time sleeping at night 'cause I had really bad dreams, but now that I'm running so much, I fall right asleep and don't remember my dreams at all.

JARVIS: What? Maybe I haven't been running enough. I'll go with you! I've been having this dream over and over where a bear's chasing me, and I run and run, but I can't get away, and he's getting closer and he has huge claws, and his mouth is dripping blood, and he knows my name. He can talk. I don't know why. And for some reason, I think that he wants to punish me for not cleaning my room. I don't know why. So now I don't even want to fall asleep. And I'm not about to clean my room because a bear told me to because—as if bears are tidy! So, I run all the time. Just in case. There have been stories about bears escaping from the zoo, so it could happen. And I'm going to be prepared. When that bear comes for me, I'll run so fast, he won't even know where I've gone. Then I'll kill him and wear his fur as a winter coat.

LARS: That would look really stupid.

JARVIS: And one more thing. No one will ever mess with me because I killed a bear!

CAMERON: You know that's kind of strange, don't you, Jarvis?

JARVIS: Maybe. But it's a good thing to be faster than a bear anyway.

EMMA: You really think a bear is going to escape from a zoo and come here?

RACHEL: That is really scary.

CAMERON: That would totally not happen.

LINDSEY: But you never know. It could!

JARVIS: And I can run faster than bears.

EMMA: How do you know?

JARVIS: I timed myself.

LARS: Not. It's not possible.

LINDSEY: Rachel, we don't run for speed.

RACHEL: Maybe we should try to run really fast today. Just for fun.

EMMA: Just in case Jarvis is right!

LINDSEY: It's better to be safe than sorry, right?

LARS: I can't believe this.

JARVIS: So are you guys coming, too?

LARS: OK. I don't care.

CAMERON: We already raced twice. I did my running for the day.

LARS: Only you didn't run.

CAMERON: Mentally I did it.

LARS: You make me look energetic!

CAMERON: Maybe I'll catch up with you guys later.

EMMA: If the bears don't catch up with you first!

Scene 2: Nightmare

JARVIS: I've never been out here.

EMMA: It's nice, isn't it? Peaceful.

JARVIS: Bears live in caves, right?

RACHEL: There aren't any bears in these caves or my dad would not have us jog out here.

LINDSEY: Have you ever explored around here like this?

RACHEL: Not really. We usually run right back.

LINDSEY: It's so dark.

EMMA: I think I see something.

JARVIS: Maybe we should go. I don't want you girls getting hurt.

(LARS enters the cave.)

LARS: This place is cool!

EMMA: Look, a big box!

LARS: What?

EMMA: Over here.

LINDSEY: Be careful.

RACHEL: Maybe we shouldn't disturb it. We don't know who it belongs to.

(EMMA, LARS, LINDSEY, and RACHEL gather around the box.)

LARS: It looks like a treasure chest.

EMMA: Do you think there could be treasure inside?

JARVIS: Maybe we should keep running. I feel like my heart needs to run right now.

LINDSEY: Open it!

RACHEL: I thought you didn't think we should.

LINDSEY: But now I want to know. And if Lars's finger-prints are on it, no one will arrest *us*.

RACHEL: Open it, Lars.

EMMA: I'll open it! *(Beat.)* It's too hard. Help me, Lars.

(LARS and EMMA try to open the box.)

HARVEY: *(From offstage.)* I wouldn't do that if I were you.

RACHEL: Who was that?

HARVEY: *(From offstage.)* I *said* I wouldn't do that if I were you.

JARVIS: Guys?

(HARVEY comes onstage. He's a giant, human-sized lizard. You can tell by the comb on his back.)

HARVEY: Hey! Seriously! Stop it! That's my stuff!

JARVIS: Guys? How fast do lizards run?

(LARS, EMMA, RACHEL, and LINDSEY turn around.)

LINDSEY: Oh my God. You're a giant lizard.

HARVEY: Thanks for the news flash. I know what I am.

RACHEL: So—so this is your stuff?

HARVEY: You got it, kid. Boy, and people say humans aren't smart.

LARS: Who says that?

HARVEY: Oh, you know. Lizards.

EMMA: Lizards aren't that smart. Usually.

HARVEY: That's what you think! Just because we don't bother under normal circumstances to speak to humans in your language, people think we're stupid. Who's stupid now, huh? I think it might be you. You—you—you *children* with your meddling and your peanut butter and jelly sandwiches. You're disgusting. Do you know the entire animal kingdom thinks you're unbearably messy? And dimwitted? It's true! Not to mention how you meddle in other people's things. Always poking around with your TV cameras and filming our private moments. Can't I just climb a tree in peace? Now this is my home. So I think you should leave, and I definitely think you should take your hands off my booty.

LARS: Your booty?

LINDSEY: Our hands are not on your booty.

HARVEY: *(Indicating LARS and EMMA.)* Their hands are.

RACHEL: Your *booty?*

HARVEY: Yes! What they have their hands on! My booty! My treasure! My life savings!

EMMA: Oooh. Your booty is your treasure.

HARVEY: Duh. You should know it's cursed.

LARS: I bet it's not. Lizards can't curse things.

HARVEY: They can't talk either, can they?

LINDSEY: He's got you there.

EMMA: I'm not touching! Please don't curse me!

JARVIS: Wait, wait, wait. Back up. The animal kingdom thinks we're messy? So . . . bears think we're messy?

HARVEY: Bears think you're unbearable. No pun intended.

JARVIS: My dream might be true. I might be psychic. And . . . can bears talk, too?

HARVEY: We can all talk in our own languages and several others. Your language is ridiculously easy.

LARS: So how come I do so badly in English?

HARVEY: Do you really want me to answer that, human?

LINDSEY: I had no idea animals were smart.

HARVEY: Well, now you know. Get outta here.

LARS: I still want to know what's inside here.

HARVEY: Go ahead. But don't say I didn't warn you.

LINDSEY: No, Lars, don't do it!

RACHEL: Don't be stupid. You don't even know what the curse is!

EMMA: What if you die?

LARS: Will I die?

HARVEY: No.

LARS: I won't die.

LINDSEY: So what will happen?

HARVEY: If I tell you, it takes all the fun out of it. But trust me, you'll be cursed.

LARS: Jarvis, help me out here.

JARVIS: No thanks.

LARS: But we could be famous! We could be on TV for

having found the lizard's treasure, and we could make a movie.

HARVEY: You people and your movies.

JARVIS: Pass. I've got a bear to worry about.

HARVEY: If you can outrun a bear, you can outrun a lizard.

JARVIS: No way. Pass. The animal kingdom has it out for me.

LARS: Chicken.

JARVIS: Yes, probably chickens, too.

LARS: How about you opening it, lizard, sir?

HARVEY: My name is Harvey. And I'm not opening it for you. I know what's inside.

LARS: Please? I just want to know. Are you rich?

HARVEY: Do I look rich? But I do have things that are important to me.

LARS: And I'm not going to die if I open it?

HARVEY: You'll just be cursed.

LARS: I'm doing it.

EMMA: No!

(With effort, LARS opens the box.)

LARS: Ew. It's just trash.

HARVEY: One man's trash is another lizard's treasure.

LARS: I feel fine.

HARVEY: Are you sure?

LARS: I think so.

LINDSEY: So what's the curse?

HARVEY: You'll find out.

(Beat while all stare at LARS.)

LARS: I really feel OK.

(LARS scratches himself.)

HARVEY: Ah-ha! It's begun.

RACHEL: What?

(LARS scratches again.)

LARS: I'm a little itchy.

HARVEY: A little itchy? A little itchy?

LARS: Yeah, a little itchy.

HARVEY: Behold! The curse of the lizard!

LARS: Oh. OK.

HARVEY: That'll teach you.

RACHEL: My mom has some calamine lotion.

LARS: Great. Thanks.

HARVEY: Let this be a lesson to you!

LARS: You bet.

EMMA: Sorry about this.

LINDSEY: I've learned a lot. Thanks. I just never knew animals were so intelligent. I'm going to look at my cat in a whole new way.

HARVEY: Cats are stupid.

LINDSEY: Oh.

JARVIS: So when I go, watch me run and let me know if I'm faster than a bear, OK?

HARVEY: No.

JARVIS: Oh. OK.

HARVEY: Well, I hope you learned a lesson today.

LARS: I learned many lessons today, sir, that I will carry with me for the rest of my life. First of all, dreams can come true. Or maybe I should say *nightmares* can come true. And it is good to be faster than a bear because you never know when a bear will chase you. Hey—doughnuts can't chase you, can they?

HARVEY: Man, you kids are dumb.

LARS: Well, that's a relief. I had this dream . . .
Anyway, animals and amphibians can talk, they just
choose not to most of the time—at least in English.
Booty also means treasure. Not just a big behind.
And if you open a huge, talking lizard's treasure
chest, as I have done today, you can expect to be
cursed. The curse will not kill you, but it will make
you itch, so you'd better have some calamine lotion
on hand. Lizards like trash. What looks to me like
a bunch of smelly, old junk is like diamonds to you.
Boy, you would think you died and went to heaven
if you went through the garbage cans behind my
house. Hey, maybe you could release me of my
curse if I brought you more booty!

HARVEY: No. Get lost.

LARS: OK.

LINDSEY: Bye!

(RACHEL, EMMA, LINDSEY, LARS, and JARVIS
exit.)

TALK BACK!

1. Did you ever do anything out of curiosity you knew you weren't supposed to do? Why?

2. Have you ever felt cursed? Why?

3. If animals could talk, what do you think they'd say?

4. What is your biggest nightmare?

5. Do you have any fears that don't make any sense? What can you do to overcome them?

DISCOVERY

3F, 3M

WHO

FEMALES   MALES
    Penelope   Alastair
    Serena   Roger
    Thea   Rupert

WHERE England.

WHEN 1910.

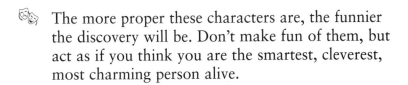 The more proper these characters are, the funnier the discovery will be. Don't make fun of them, but act as if you think you are the smartest, cleverest, most charming person alive.

I've always wondered how people discover they can do silly and bizarre things with their bodies. How in the world does someone discover he can make his eyes pop out of his head? Is it an accident? Write a play about the day early humans discovered they could walk upright.

Scene 1: Picnic

ROGER: Good day, ladies.

THEA: Good day, Roger.

SERENA: Do join us.

ROGER: I don't mind if I do. What a lovely picnic you've set up here.

PENELOPE: I'm afraid we ate most of it.

ROGER: No matter. I've already had my tea.

(ALASTAIR and RUPERT enter.)

ALASTAIR: I say! What do we have here?

RUPERT: What a cozy picture.

THEA: We've been having a very nice time.

SERENA: Do join us.

RUPERT: I can't speak for Alistair here, but I certainly shall.

ALASTAIR: As will I. Lovely day!

PENELOPE: Absolutely!

ROGER: The weather is fine, is it not?

ALASTAIR: That is precisely what I was implying.

ROGER: Ah, of course, old chap.

SERENA: He's not actually old, is he?

ROGER: Not at all, just a figure of speech.

RUPERT: What does that mean, "a figure of speech"?

THEA: Well, it's just a way of saying something.

RUPERT: But there's really no figure involved at all, is there?

PENELOPE: You're right.

THEA: How interesting!

SERENA: I don't understand.

(Beat.)

ALASTAIR: You ate most of the food already.

PENELOPE: Yes. Sorry.

ALASTAIR: No matter.

(Beat.)

RUPERT: So!

(ALL turn to look at RUPERT. Beat.)

RUPERT: Well! I . . . What I was going to say slipped my mind, I'm afraid. Sorry.

ALASTAIR: No matter.

SERENA: I say!

(All turn expectantly to look at SERENA. Beat.)

SERENA: Is that a squirrel?

ROGER: I believe it is!

THEA: Quite astounding!

PENELOPE: Yes, there he is!

(Beat.)

ALASTAIR: So what were you speaking about before Rupert and I came along, Roger?

ROGER: Well, there was . . .

RUPERT: Yes . . .

ROGER: That I had had my tea . . .

ALASTAIR: Yes . . .

RUPERT: And . . .

ROGER: That's it.

ALASTAIR: Oh.

PENELOPE: You came along right after he arrived.

RUPERT: How strange!

ALASTAIR: Providential!

ROGER: Indeed!

THEA: Now here we are, all together, on such a fine day.

PENELOPE: Yes!

RUPERT: Quite.

ROGER: Indeed!

SERENA: Jolly right.

ALASTAIR: Just so!

(Long beat. PENELOPE looks at the sky, ALASTAIR looks at the grass, SERENA examines her nails, ROGER straightens his clothes, THEA looks at the others nervously, and RUPERT looks like he's concentrating.)

RUPERT: *(Suddenly.)* Oh dear Lord!

THEA: What is it?

RUPERT: I've just . . . I've discovered something!

PENELOPE: Whatever can it be?

RUPERT: Well, I don't know if I can say . . .

SERENA: Do say, Rupert.

THEA: Please?

ALASTAIR: We'd all like to know.

ROGER: Out with it, old chap!

RUPERT: Well, you see . . . I can do something. That is my discovery.

SERENA: What is it that you can do?

RUPERT: I don't know if I ought—

ALASTAIR: Go on then.

ROGER: Out with it!

RUPERT: Since you insist . . .

(RUPERT curls his tongue. PENELOPE lets out a blood-curdling scream. SERENA faints. THEA covers her eyes.)

THEA: Why did you have to do that? I think I'm blind!

(ROGER fans SERENA.)

ROGER: See what you've done, you beast!

(ALASTAIR embraces PENELOPE.)

ALASTAIR: Everything is going to be all right, darling.

PENELOPE: How can you be sure?

ROGER: I say, what were you thinking?

RUPERT: Terribly sorry, I just suddenly discovered I could curl my tongue. Is it really so odd?

(SERENA *slowly awakens as the next few lines are said.*)

ROGER: Well, I don't know. I've never seen anything like that.

PENELOPE: I hope I never shall again.

THEA: It's just so . . . curious.

PENELOPE: Freakish! I'm sorry to say so, but it's true!

RUPERT: Well, it feels quite natural. Can you not do it?

ROGER: Well, of course not!

RUPERT: How do you know?

ROGER: Very well, I'll prove it!

(ROGER *curls his tongue.* PENELOPE *screams;* SERENA, *now awake, faints again;* THEA *covers her eyes.*)

ROGER: Oh, good Lord! I, too, am a freak.

PENELOPE: It's too horrible!

THEA: I cannot look! I am afraid to see ever again!

ALASTAIR: I hate to be the bearer of bad news, but there's no other choice. I'm afraid you two must now join the circus.

ROGER: You don't mean . . .

ALASTAIR: I'm afraid so.

RUPERT: Isn't that a bit extreme?

PENELOPE: No! It is only right!

RUPERT: But is there nothing at all unusual you are able to do?

ALASTAIR: Nothing at all. I am perfectly normal.

(SERENA awakens.)

RUPERT: But can you not . . . cross your eyes?

(PENELOPE screams; SERENA faints; THEA covers her eyes.)

THEA: No! Please don't!

ALASTAIR: My God, this is even more dire than I originally thought. Please, go, before you cause any more distress!

ROGER: Come on, old chap. There's no fighting it.

RUPERT: But—

ROGER: **We must face it. We are hideous freaks. There's no getting around it. We can do something strange with our bodies that other people cannot, would not, could not, should not. We belong behind bars. In a cage. Locked up! Standing beside all the bearded ladies, lizard boys, and elephant men. We** are—tongue curlers. Please, everyone, stay calm. We mean no harm. We will go willingly, peacefully. I confess I am sorry to go, but go I shall. Though we share the same fate and must somehow get along, I must say I am very sorry to know you, Rupert. Were it not for you and your experimentations and discoveries, I might still think of myself as normal. I might be able to hide my deformity and live a regular life! You have taken that from me. And for that, I shall never forgive you, though I stand at your side, a fellow freak. Curse you, tongue curler!

(SERENA awakens.)

RUPERT: I say, I was just fooling around. It was nothing really. I don't know why you are all so upset by this. I cannot for one moment believe that none of the rest of you has any other oddities about you. Why, besides tongue curling, I can cross my eyes, hop on one foot, and get my bird, Doodle, to eat out of my mouth!

THEA: No more! I beg you!

RUPERT: Honestly, don't any of you experiment with what you are able to do at all?

ALASTAIR: I should say not!

RUPERT: Never turned your eyelids inside out? Never tried to pop your eyes out of your head? Never made only one eyebrow go up or walked on your hands?

ROGER: Why would anyone want to try those things?

PENELOPE: Truly bizarre!

RUPERT: Haven't you any curiosity? Don't you get bored?

SERENA: You need to be behind bars!

ALASTAIR: Come, come! You're upsetting the ladies.

ROGER: We must accept our fate, friend.

RUPERT: But I don't!

ROGER: You must.

THEA: I am sorry, dear Rupert, that it had to end this way. I loved you, truly I did. But now . . . it can never be. For you are a freak. It pains me even to say it! I had always dreamed of living a perfectly perfect life with you. Filled to the brim with normalcy. We would wake in the morning normally, breakfast normally, walk about the house normally—what a beautiful life it would have been. But now . . . it cannot be! As I speak I can feel my heart breaking into little, tiny, pointy pieces. The pain, Rupert! All because you could not leave well enough alone. Now we both must pay the price. Don't you see the folly of your ways? How you've injured me forever and ever? I may never get over this. Oh sure, I will drink tea and walk in the park and do needlepoint as I always do. I may even marry another. I hope you see that may be necessary. I cannot bind myself to a circus freak. But there will always be a part of me . . .

(THEA breaks down, dissolving into tears.)

SERENA: You mustn't cry, dearest. Everything will turn

out all right. For you, anyway. You're not a freak. Are you?

ROGER: Let us go, Rupert.

RUPERT: Very well. I hope you will visit us when the circus comes to town.

ALISTAIR: Perhaps so.

PENELOPE: I am very sorry for you.

ROGER: It has been an enchanting afternoon, ladies and gents. Filled with discoveries. Farewell.

Scene 2: Circus

(Large sign advertises "Horrifying Tongue Curlers!")

BARKER: Step right up, step right up and see the terrify-ing, the horrifying, the gosh-darn unbelievable twin Tongue Curlers if you dare. Who would think there would be two such freaks in all the world! Not I, ladies and gents, not I. Hold onto your ladies; hold onto your hats. This sight is not for the faint of heart! Step up; step up now. Pay your money and see the horrifying Tongue Curlers!

PENELOPE: I can't believe we're here.

ALASTAIR: We told them we'd come by to see them.

SERENA: I'm frightened.

THEA: But we've already seen them once. You needn't be afraid. It will be no different than before.

SERENA: I know it, but I'm still frightened. What if Rupert does something hideous, like cross his eyes at the same time!

ALASTAIR: You mustn't think such things.

THEA: We are their friends. We must be brave.

PENELOPE: They are no friends of mine. I find them disgusting.

THEA: Penelope, really!

PENELOPE: Well, I'm sorry if you don't like it, but it's

true. It's what we're all thinking. I can't believe I used to socialize with these beasts.

THEA: They are still people, Penny!

PENELOPE: Thea, look around you! These so-called people are freaks. Freaks! They no longer belong to our social strata.

THEA: Don't you think we ought to look at these poor creatures with pity? Why, what if Serena here was born with a pig's nose.

SERENA: I haven't got a pig's nose! I've got a very nice nose. My daddy told me so.

ALASTAIR: Of course you do, my dear.

THEA: It was just an example.

SERENA: But my nose is nice! How dare you say something so uncharitable, Thea!

THEA: I didn't mean—

PENELOPE: Yes, yes. It's a very nice nose, Serena. Now back to—

SERENA: If you were to compare my nose to an animal, it would have to be a swan or something quite beautiful. Isn't that so, Alastair?

THEA: Serena, enough! I didn't mean it. I apologize. Your nose looks absolutely nothing like a pig's.

SERENA: I've got the nose of a goddess.

PENELOPE: Let's drop the nose, please!

SERENA: Drop my nose? I'm not a leper. My nose is attached.

PENELOPE: Thea, were you saying something?

THEA: Very well. Say *my* nose was like a pig's.

SERENA: Well, that makes more sense. It is a bit.

THEA: No, it's not! Serena, how horrid of you!

SERENA: You're angry at *me*? You were the one who started with the pig-nose thing.

THEA: It was merely a hypothetical example.

SERENA: There is nothing historical about it! None of my relatives ever had pig noses! My Aunt Petunia had a most peculiar nose, I'll admit, but—

ALASTAIR: No, my dear. Hypothetical means that it's an imaginary example used merely to prove a point.

SERENA: Well, what's the point?

PENELOPE: Finally!

THEA: The point is, we are best friends. But would you hate me if I was born . . . unusual?

PENELOPE: Indubitably.

THEA: Really? What about you Serena?

SERENA: Like Penelope said, dubiously.

ALASTAIR: That's not actually what she said, love.

THEA: What about you, Alastair?

ALASTAIR: Well, I don't imagine we'd know you if you were born with a—were you not as you are today.

PENELOPE: Very true!

BARKER: Now, for your spine-tingling pleasure, the Tongue Curlers!

(SERENA faints.)

PENELOPE: Serena, they haven't even come out yet.

SERENA: Oh.

(SERENA stands. ROGER and RUPERT come onstage.)

SERENA: They look exactly the same.

PENELOPE: Of course.

SERENA: I thought they would wear a costume or something.

ALASTAIR: It makes their deformity all the more bizarre and terrifying. They appear to be just like us.

SERENA: I never would have guessed they'd be freaks.

PENELOPE: Serena, you saw them firsthand when their . . . oddness first became apparent.

ROGER: I say, look, Rupert! Our dear . . .

(ALASTAIR, PENELOPE, SERENA, and THEA look around them awkwardly, pretending they don't know ROGER and RUPERT.)

ROGER: Ah, yes. Of course.

RUPERT: You're going to pretend you don't know us?

THEA: Oh, Rupert, I don't want to! But what would people say?

RUPERT: Who cares what people say? I'll have you know there are quite a few women who find me attractive, despite the tongue curling!

PENELOPE: What women are those? The bearded ladies?

ROGER: As a matter of fact, yes! The snake charmer as well. She can charm more than just snakes, I must say.

ALASTAIR: There are ladies about, Roger!

ROGER: Apologies.

RUPERT: **There are also noncircus folk who enjoy my stunning personality. I've traveled the world over. I'm handsome, debonair, sophisticated, and well traveled. What's not to like?**

PENELOPE: The tongue . . . thing.

RUPERT: I must tell you we went over very well in the East. There men charm cobras, walk on hot coals, do all kinds of bizarre and amazing things. The human body is quite remarkable. We are all—you included—capable of simply astonishing feats! Your inability to see this saddens me. It is too pathetic of educated people like yourselves. Every time I discover something new about myself, I confess I am driven to discover more. It is so exciting! You are missing so much. I find our bodies fascinating. Why there is a man in Africa who can swallow swords! Astonishing! When a man is unique, he feels as though he has a place in the world. He is set apart from the masses. I am glad, even proud, of being a tongue curler! I shall curl my tongue 'til I die and be damned happy to do it!

ALASTAIR: Rupert! Watch your language! The ladies!

PENELOPE: Well, you have a show to do and we . . . need to . . . go. Now.

ALASTAIR: Of course, my dear. Well, good to . . . (*Loudly.*) meet for the very first time ever in our lives, gentlemen!

ROGER: Right! Cheerio!

ALASTAIR: Ladies, shall we go?

(*ALASTAIR, PENELOPE, SERENA, and THEA turn to leave.*)

THEA: Wait!

SERENA: Am I stepping on your dress?

THEA: No. I can't go.

PENELOPE: Why?

THEA: Because—I can't leave you, Rupert!

RUPERT: Dear girl! Then you'll join me in my travels?

THEA: Are you asking . . .

RUPERT: Marry me!

THEA: Yes, Rupert, yes! I thought you'd never ask! Let's go freaking everywhere as man and wife!

ROGER: Well, this is good news.

SERENA: I believe I've learned something.

ROGER: What's that?

SERENA: People in Africa have sore throats.

ROGER: No, swords in their throats.

SERENA: That's what I said.

ROGER: Ah. Yes. Jolly good. Well, I hope you two are very happy. As for me, I no longer wish to be a freak. I believe I will go into hiding. Perhaps move to France. I like cheese; that should work out well. For you see, I've discovered that I can choose *not* to act freakishly. If I never do anything untoward and always act normally, no one will ever know my secret. My travels have shown me that I very much like girls. Previously, I was so busy drinking tea day and night that I found myself in the lavatory more often than not. I never had time to actually pay attention to females. However, now I plan to meet a lot of them. From all sorts of backgrounds. Though I don't share Rupert's fascination for oddities, I do share a love of diversity. Did you know that girls come in all shapes, sizes, and colors? It's quite stimulating. I wish to meet them all. So long as I stay away from tea, I think I may be able to accomplish this. Wish me luck!

SERENA: Luck!

PENELOPE: Serena, don't!

SERENA: I think I need a rest. This whole day has been very confusing.

ALASTAIR: Yes, your brain has been increasingly addled since this incident. Let's go, ladies. Farewell, Thea and Rupert. May you be happy. And Roger, wish the girls well for me.

PENELOPE: Alastair!

ALASTAIR: Well, off we go!

THEA: We plan to be happy.

ROGER: And I shall get the freak out of here. Me, that is.

SERENA: Did this end well?

ALASTAIR: I believe so.

SERENA: Good.

BARKER: Excuse me, but I couldn't help wondering . . .
(To SERENA.) My dear, how would you like to be the
Amazing Brainless Woman?

SERENA: I am amazing . . .

TALK BACK!

1. Freak shows were very popular for many years. Why?

2. How do people discover they have bizarre talents?

3. Why do people like to gross each other out by doing things like showing wounds and bending their limbs in the wrong direction?

4. What do you think of Penelope? Is she a snob? Can you justify her desire not to be seen with Rupert and Roger in Scene 2?

5. What is the definition of normal?

6. What makes a person a freak?

7. John Merrick, a.k.a. "the elephant man," was often treated poorly and feared for his deformed appearance (due to a rare disease). How do you honestly think you'd react if confronted with someone with a truly bizarre appearance?

ACTOR!

5M

WHO
    MALES
        Aaron
        Bruce
        Elijah
        Tom Hanks
        Trent

WHERE Aaron's living room.

WHEN Present day.

🎭 Aaron has to be as convincing as possible. All actors must make sure they don't "play the end." In other words, you must be unsure of Aaron's motives and whether he's telling the truth until the very end.

✎ Write a play about a big, huge lie. Make it as outrageous and unbelievable as you like.

Scene 1: Brush with Death

AARON: Oh my God. You will never believe what happened to me yesterday, you guys.

TRENT: A supermodel fell in love with you?

ELIJAH: You were asked to be on a professional football team?

BRUCE: You did the stunts on a Tom Cruise movie?

AARON: You guys are so dumb. I nearly got killed.

BRUCE: Uh-huh.

TRENT: Wow, man. That's heavy.

AARON: Yeah! I was on the bus and the bus driver stops suddenly, right?

ELIJAH: Right. So does anyone want to get some chili cheese fries?

AARON: I'm talking here! About my almost-death! So, anyway, the driver just stops. And everyone's like "What's going on?" Some people go to the front of the bus, but I'm thinking it's just traffic. Or an accident. Why do people want to look at accidents? If I'm lying on the street with my brains hanging out, I don't exactly want people to be looking at just that moment. Not to mention that then everyone complains about how bad the traffic is, but they were the ones that messed it up by slowing down to look. And how boring is a low speed police chase? Why do they show them on TV? I'd rather watch anything! Even those TV movies my mom watches where there's always a woman who's husband secretly had an affair and now he wants to kill her so he can be with the new sexy woman—Hey, why are all those TV movies exactly the same? When my mom watches them, I tell her what's going to happen at the end: the wife is going to have to kill her husband and then she'll stand trial and she'll get off right at the very end and her life will go back to normal. Bor-ing.

TRENT: What are you talking about?

BRUCE: Do you like those shows?

AARON: No way! That's what I'm saying!

ELIJAH: Sounds like you like them.

AARON: I don't like them. Anyway—

TRENT: Sure sounds like you like them.

AARON: I don't like them, OK? **ANYWAY, as I was saying, the bus driver stops, everybody looks, and there's this silence. Then the driver says really quiet, "Murder." Just like that! Really quiet. Everyone gets really still. Then the bus driver starts saying, again really quiet, "oh my God" over and over again.**

ELIJAH: If he was quiet, how did you hear him?

AARON: **You guys are so dumb.** *Everyone* **was quiet. That's how I heard the bus driver. So the bus driver is like "oh my God, oh my God" and he starts** backing up the bus. And I'm thinking, we're going to hit other cars! The road is really narrow, right? So I'm thinking we have to turn this bus around and go forward, but there's no room—

BRUCE: And you didn't die. The end.

AARON: Bruce, shut up!

TRENT: I almost want to hear what comes next now.

AARON: Thanks, Trent. Yeah, so, the bus is backing up and I look behind us, and there are cars. I want to look ahead and see how the bus driver knows there was a murder. So I peek above my seat. I don't want to get shot or anything. I'm not crazy or anything! So I look up and there's this guy looking at the bus. And there's a body at his feet and a gun in his hand. He's looking at the bus. Then slowly, like in slow motion, he raises his hand. The gun hand.

ELIJAH: Then he shot the bus driver and you had to drive the bus and the guy shot at you, too, but you got away.

AARON: Did you see this on the news?

BRUCE: The news! That's a great idea. A story like that has got to be in the news.

AARON: What do you mean? There's loads of crimes. It might not be.

TRENT: A kid driving a bus? A guy gets shot? A crazy killer on the loose?

AARON: Well, also one of the people on the bus got shot, too.

ELIJAH: A man or a woman?

AARON: A woman. Well, not exactly. She was like a college student. We were talking on the bus before she died.

BRUCE: I thought you said everyone was quiet.

AARON: So dumb, I swear. *Before* everyone was quiet that girl was talking to me on the bus.

TRENT: *She* was talking to *you*.

AARON: Well, yeah. She wasn't foreign or anything.

ELIJAH: Foreign people can talk.

AARON: I didn't mean foreign. I meant deaf.

BRUCE: Yeah, those words sound the same.

AARON: I wasn't thinking. Because I was remembering that she *was* foreign when I was talking just then. Because she was.

TRENT: So where was she from?

AARON: Um, Sweden.

BRUCE: Is this bothering anyone else?

ELIJAH: I'm just wondering when this story is going to end.

TRENT: We were gonna turn on the TV so we could see this story on the news. Dude, maybe you should go home! I bet TV stations and stuff are calling your house.

ELIJAH: And the police must want to talk to you.

AARON: Oh, yeah. It's covered.

ELIJAH: What's covered?

AARON: I talked to the police.

TRENT: When did this happen?

AARON: A couple of hours ago.

BRUCE: I thought it was yesterday.

AARON: Exactly. A couple of hours ago yesterday. You have to let me finish what I'm saying, Bruce.

BRUCE: Are you serious?

AARON: Dude, being shot at is as serious as it gets.

BRUCE: Look, I've had it! You were not shot at. You didn't drive a bus. It's a lie. It's all a lie. Why do you lie all the time, Aaron? It's annoying.

TRENT: Don't be too hard on him. It's kinda funny.

BRUCE: It's not funny. Or cute. Or interesting. And it's not at all believable. Do you really think we buy this crap? You must really think we *are* dumb. But we're not. You're the one that's dumb. You're just making an idiot of yourself. You can't even keep your lies straight! You don't ever know if someone tried to kill you yesterday or today!

AARON: I told you—

BRUCE: Shut up, Aaron! Seriously! I've had it. I don't want to be your friend anymore. You're an idiot. It was funny when we were kids, but not anymore. Now I'm embarrassed to know you. Have you ever said anything honest in your whole life?

AARON: Duh—

BRUCE: Don't say "duh." And don't call me dumb. I'm smart, OK? Smart! Get a clue! Seriously, Aaron, I'm sorry to say all this, but it's what I think. Unless you can admit to me now that you lied, I'm out of here.

AARON: It did happen.

BRUCE: Then why don't you want us to watch the news?

AARON: I hate the news. It's boring.

BRUCE: Even if you're on it?

TRENT: Come on, Bruce. Back off a little.

BRUCE: Why? I'm just telling the truth. At least *someone* here is telling the truth.

ELIJAH: Yeah, but he's just being a goof. You're being cruel.

AARON: What are you talking about?

BRUCE: He's not being a goof. Look at him. He honestly thinks we don't know. He thinks you take him seriously.

AARON: You don't believe me? You guys are so—

BRUCE: Don't say it.

TRENT: You're cool, Aaron. Don't worry about it.

BRUCE: Don't encourage him!

TRENT: Why not? He's our friend.

BRUCE: You're picking him over me?

ELIJAH: He's funny.

BRUCE: He's a liar! And he won't even admit it!

ELIJAH: Maybe he believes it.

AARON: You guys! I'm totally serious. Go ahead! Turn on the news. You'll see.

Scene 2: Brush with Fame

BRUCE: Oh my God, it did happen! You were shot at and people died and you drove a bus and saved a bunch of people yesterday.

AARON: Told you.

TRENT: So that time you said you were able to fly?

AARON: Um, yeah. I was five. You say things when you're five.

ELIJAH: But they didn't say anything about a Swedish college student getting shot in the news story.

BRUCE: And no way did a college girl like you.

AARON: I didn't say she liked me; I said she talked to me.

BRUCE: So some cute Swedish college girl who's like eighteen or whatever was talking to you on the bus.

AARON: I didn't say how old she was.

BRUCE: Ah-ha! She was old!

AARON: She wasn't old.

BRUCE: You made it seem like she was.

AARON: You are so dumb.

ELIJAH: Was she really Swedish?

AARON: I don't know. That's what she said.

TRENT: So last week when you said you won a trip to go on safari in Africa but you're parents wouldn't let you go, that was true?

AARON: Guys, seriously, these questions are stupid. And I have another story to tell you.

BRUCE: Where did you learn to drive so you could save those people on the bus?

AARON: I didn't. I just used my instincts. You know, one time Tom Hanks told me I had great instincts.

(Beat.)

BRUCE: Tom Hanks. You're saying not only did you meet Tom Hanks, but that he complimented you on your "great instincts."

AARON: Well, you don't need to get your hearing checked.

TRENT: When did you meet Tom Hanks?

AARON: When I was in Hollywood.

ELIJAH: When were you in Hollywood.

AARON: Oh, I don't know. The summer.

BRUCE: So why did Tom Hanks tell you that you have great instincts?

AARON: Oh, it's a silly story. You don't want to hear it, Bruce.

TRENT: Now see, Bruce. You ruined it for the rest of us.

BRUCE: Fine. I can admit when I'm wrong. I'm sorry I called you a liar before. It's just that you say so many outrageous things; it's impossible to believe you.

AARON: That was an apology?

ELIJAH: You have to admit, you're a little dramatic. And you have been known to . . . exaggerate, shall we say?

AARON: Elijah, I'm surprised at you. I thought—

TRENT: Aaron, just get on with the story.

AARON: Fine. So I'm in Hollywood walking around and there's Tom Hanks. And I say, "Tom Hanks!"

ELIJAH: Very original.

AARON: And Tom Hanks is like, "Kid on the street!" So that was funny. And I say I love his movies, and he's a great actor. And he says, "Kid on the street, you've got great instincts."

TRENT: That's believable.

AARON: Well, yeah. Duh. So then I tell him my name and he wants me to be in his next movie. And I'm so excited, right, because I'm going to play a spy. I tell him about my work on the Tom Cruise film as a stunt man—

BRUCE: That so did not happen. No way did that happen!

TRENT: Don't interrupt!

AARON: And Tom Hanks says to me, "Kid, you are very impressive for one so young."

ELIJAH: So how come you didn't do the movie?

BRUCE: Tom Hanks wanted you to play *a spy*? You're a kid. Kids aren't spies.

TRENT: Not officially, but lots of kids probably are spies unofficially. No one would suspect a kid.

AARON: Exactly!

ELIJAH: So, about the movie?

AARON: Oh. My parents wouldn't let me because it would have gone into the school year.

BRUCE: So Tom Hanks meets you on the street and suddenly wants to give you a Hollywood role.

AARON: I guess so.

BRUCE: Don't they have people who cast movies? Tom Hanks doesn't do that. It's not his job.

AARON: Dude, he's a Hollywood star. He can do whatever he wants. He could go into your house and steal your TV right in front of everyone, and he wouldn't get arrested.

ELIJAH: Why not?

AARON: That's the way it is.

BRUCE: No, it's not!

TRENT: So you won a safari in Africa, too?

ELIJAH: Your parents are harsh if they won't let you do this cool stuff.

AARON: They're always like, "Your education is too important." It is *too* important. Who needs a school education? I want *life* education!

ELIJAH: I guess that argument doesn't work.

BRUCE: So can I have this safari vacation then?

AARON: No.

BRUCE: Why not? Did you give it to your friend Derek Jeter?

AARON: Because you're mean, that's why. Plus, Derek Jeter can just go on safari whenever he wants so long as it's not during baseball season.

TRENT: You're so busted, Bruce. So, can I have it?

AARON: I had to give it back already, sorry.

TRENT: It's all right.

ELIJAH: Wait a sec. You said once that you played pro football.

AARON: Right. So?

ELIJAH: So you played pro football?

AARON: Why are you guys questioning me all of a sudden?

ELIJAH: To be honest, we all thought you were lying all of the time. We'd just wait to see what crazy thing came out of your mouth next. Did you perform open-heart surgery in a taxi? Did you find a leprechaun in your basement? Did you win a million dollars in Vegas?

AARON: Yes, yes, and yes.

ELIJAH: Can't you hear how crazy and unbelievable all of that sounds? Leprechauns? How are we supposed know when to believe you? Especially when you won't admit when it's a joke. You were never a vampire on *Buffy the Vampire Slayer*. You were, like, way too young and you were in school when you said you were filming the scene! You actually said to me, "Oh, I filmed it on Wednesday," and were in school that day! *And* you came over my house and played video games and had dinner with my family that night, so you can't say you did it after school. So how are we supposed to know when something's true? How are we supposed to trust you if it's important? What if we were on that bus with you when you were being shot at yesterday? If you told me to get down so I didn't get shot, I'd laugh at you. And I guess I'd be dead. How can we tell when you're actually being serious?

AARON: OK. Want to know the truth?

BRUCE: I've been begging you!

AARON: I've been preparing for a film.

BRUCE: Here we go again.

AARON: I need to play a liar in this film and I've been preparing. So sometimes I need to lie to get into my role.

ELIJAH: You've been preparing for a role for, like, ten years?

AARON: Well, the stuff about being able to fly and all that were just kid stuff.

TRENT: I liked it better when the lies were more fun. This one is dull.

AARON: Maybe that's because it's the truth. I wrote a book a while back, and some producers loved it, and they wanted me to make it into a screenplay and be the lead actor. I had to beg my parents to go along with it. They like the idea of me being a famous writer more than me being a famous actor. They're weird like that.

TRENT: So how come it's taking so long to start making the movie?

AARON: We're making it right now.

ELIJAH: Right now. We're making it right now.

AARON: Didn't you ever notice Ernie the cameraman? Wave to the people, Ernie.

(AARON waves to a figure offstage.)

TRENT: I always thought he was a stalker or something.

(TOM HANKS enters.)

AARON: Hey! Tom Hanks!

TOM HANKS: Hi, Aaron. Having some trouble here?

AARON: You guys, this is Tom Hanks. He's producing this documentary.

TOM HANKS: It's called *Actor! The True Story of a Habitual Liar.*

BRUCE: It's a good title.

TOM HANKS: It's going to win an Oscar!

ELIJAH: But you're not Tom Hanks. You don't look like Tom Hanks.

TOM HANKS: Oh, you mean *that* Tom Hanks. I'm not *that* Tom Hanks, but I'm Tom Hanks. By the way, the looks on your faces were priceless when we showed that fake news footage.

BRUCE: I *knew* it was a lie!

TOM HANKS: Yes, kid. You're very annoying like that.

TRENT: If it's all the same to everyone here, I'd like to pretend this conversation never took place. I liked not knowing if Aaron here was lying or not. It was exciting to think that the weird stories he told *might* somehow be true, even if I was pretty sure they weren't. It's exciting to think that your friend might be a stunt man or a racecar driver or a pilot or a scientist from the future who traveled here in a time machine. It makes me feel like my life is more exciting than the average kid's. I don't know, it's also like I feel like I can also do more stuff, too, if you know what I mean. Say you tell a story about saving a kid from drowning. I think, "If he can do that, maybe I can be a doctor when I'm older." It makes what I want to do not seem so crazy. Plus, it's funnier when it doesn't seem to be about making money and getting ahead. When it's just a goof. But I am glad that cameraman who's been following us isn't a stalker. He was freaking me out!

ELIJAH: Completely!

TRENT: So are we agreed?

BRUCE: Whatever you want, Trent.

ELIJAH: I see your point. Sometimes Aaron's lying was annoying, but it's also a lot of fun.

TOM HANKS: Kid, you're going to make it in this business with that "I don't want to know" attitude.

AARON: Just don't expect top billing.

TOM HANKS: Can I get your signatures on these contracts, boys? Then we can pretend this never happened and be big stars.

BRUCE: I guess so.

TALK BACK!

1. What motivates people to lie about themselves?

2. What's one lie you've told about yourself or something you did or did not do? Why did you do it?

3. Do you think you'd like or dislike being Aaron's friend? Why?

4. If you could tell one lie about yourself and have everyone around you believe it, what would it be?

5. The truth shall set you free. True or false?

6. Lies are interesting; the truth is boring. What do you think of this statement?

WHAT A BOY WANTS

2F, 3M

WHO

FEMALES   MALES
  Casey   Carter
  Hillary   Gerald
                      Graham

WHERE Sitting at Gerald's kitchen table.

WHEN Present day.

🎭 Comedy needs to be grounded in reality. The characters need to mean what they say. However, it also has to be bigger than life. It is an outrageous situation. Try to find the balance between being realistic and being big with your acting.

✍ Write a play about how Gerald got into his predicament. What happened to bring about this change?

Scene 1: The Change

HILLARY: Hi! Where's Geraldine? We're going to the mall.

GERALD: Don't you know me?

HILLARY: No. Are . . . are you her brother? She told me you were in college.

GERALD: Very funny, Hillary.

HILLARY: She told you about me? Hey—what's funny?

GERALD: You can stop it now.

HILLARY: Um, you're going to have to start making sense. Or could you just go get Geraldine?

GERALD: Hill.

HILLARY: I'll just go up to her room myself, OK?

GERALD: Hill!

HILLARY: You really don't know me well enough to talk to me like that.

GERALD: Hill, quit it!

HILLARY: Quit what? I think you should quit it. Is your mom at home?

GERALD: She went to the store.

HILLARY: Oh. Maybe I should go now. Tell Hillary I stopped by to see her, OK?

GERALD: Quit it, Hill. Let's go.

HILLARY: Um, I'm not going anywhere with you. I don't even know you.

GERALD: OK, OK! I'll play. It's me, Hillary. Geraldine.

HILLARY: Ha, ha, ha. Very funny.

GERALD: OK, now that we've gotten that over with, we can go now.

HILLARY: I told you, kid, I'm not going anywhere with you. *I don't know you.*

GERALD: Good God, Hillary, this is getting really boring! Stop being such a dweebie.

HILLARY: Dweebie? You called me a dweebie.

GERALD: I know. I always do.

HILLARY: But . . . always? That's what . . . Geraldine?

GERALD: That's my name, don't wear it out. It doesn't go with your skirt.

HILLARY: Oh my God! It is you! Is this . . . Oh my God that is so funny!

GERALD: What? You really are weird today, Hilly Head.

HILLARY: Are you going to a party or something?

GERALD: Should I be?

HILLARY: Well, what's the getup for?

GERALD: Hill, MAKE SENSE!

HILLARY: You cut your hair!

GERALD: No, I . . .

(GERALD touches his head.)

GERALD: Who did this to me?

HILLARY: Ger—You're freaking me out, whoever you are.

GERALD: You're freaking *me* out, Hillary!

(HILLARY pulls a mirror out of her bag.)

HILLARY: Look!

GERALD: Ah! What happened to me?

HILLARY: Are you really Geraldine or is this a joke?

GERALD: Of course I'm Geraldine, Hill!

HILLARY: Prove it.

GERALD: In first grade you wet yourself during gym class and begged me not to tell and then you pretended to fall into a puddle so no one would know. And last year, you cheated on a vocabulary test. You stuff your bra and—

HILLARY: OK! Enough! So . . . what happened to you?

GERALD: As if I know!

HILLARY: I mean, are you . . . is it just the hair?

GERALD: You mean . . . I don't know!

HILLARY: Check!

GERALD: I don't want to!

HILLARY: But if it's permanent . . .

GERALD: Don't say that! This is completely freaky. I'm scared, Hill.

HILLARY: It'll be OK.

GERALD: But . . . I have to go to the bathroom!

HILLARY: So go! Then you'll know.

GERALD: But what if . . . **I DON'T WANT TO BE A BOY! They're disgusting. And rude and horrible and . . . if I have a boy's body I will completely freak out! I mean it, Hillary. I will lose it big time. How can this be? How can this happen? I mean, I still sort of look like me, but not really. My face is sort of wider. I'm taller, aren't I? Just a little? And . . . (Touches his chest.) They're gone! I worked so hard to get them, Hill! And they disappeared! This is totally unfair. I hate this! Where's my mom?**

HILLARY: At the store, remember?

GERALD: Is this a dream? Pinch me, Hill!

(*HILLARY pinches GERALD.*)

GERALD: Ow! If this is a dream, it stinks! I want to wake up! I don't want to wear only olive green and navy blue. I want to wear pink and orange and flowers and hoop earrings, Hillary! And I guess a boy could wear those things, but he'd be beat up and he'd look like a gay pirate and I don't want to get beat up! I'm a girl! I should be a girl. Why am I not a girl, Hill? I hate sports. They are so boring. I'm going to get killed at school for sure. But maybe death is better than being a boy. My parents will cry and . . . you'll come to my funeral, right, Hill?

HILLARY: Stop it, Geraldine!

GERALD: I've got to get a grip. OK, breathe, Geraldine.

(*GERALD breathes heavily.*)

GERALD: It's useless! I can't take this!

HILLARY: When did this happen?

GERALD: I don't know. I mean, I'm pretty sure I looked like me this morning when I got dressed. I think I would have noticed then if I wasn't a girl.

HILLARY: You would think so.

GERALD: So then I just came downstairs and ate some cereal.

HILLARY: What kind?

GERALD: Does it matter?

HILLARY: I don't know.

GERALD: Cheerios.

HILLARY: No, I don't think Cheerios have magical powers. So then what?

GERALD: So then I just sat here and waited for you to come. I watched TV and I looked at the comics in the paper even though they're never funny—I don't know why I do that. And I bit my nails for a while. I know it's gross but I can't help it. And . . . I daydreamed a little . . . That's it!

HILLARY: I don't know, Geraldine. Seems like someone put a voodoo curse on you or something.

GERALD: Who would do that? I'm very likable.

HILLARY: I guess so.

GERALD: You "guess so"? I am, Hillary!

HILLARY: I know. I'm your best friend, after all. But maybe everyone doesn't think so.

GERALD: Like who?

HILLARY: Like . . . I don't know. Do you get along with your brother?

GERALD: He's way older than me. I hardly ever see him.

HILLARY: That's what I thought! When I thought maybe you were your brother, I was like, "But isn't her brother way older than her?"

GERALD: Anyway . . .

HILLARY: Well, so what about the gym teacher, Mrs. Florkabbich? She hates you.

GERALD: Just 'cause I can't play volleyball? I don't know what her problem is. Honestly, like volleyball ever saved the world. She should get a life. But do you really think she *hates* me?

HILLARY: Well, she does have kids—poor things, they must run in circles day and night—so she ought to have better things to do with her time than cursing you. But then there's Karen Murray-Hoffman-Hinkley.

GERALD: I hate Karen Murray-Hoffman-Hinkley! She told me I was fat in gym class. She's the fatty! Fatbutt Karen Murray-Hoffman-Hinkley. When she runs, the whole room shakes! Who has three last names anyway? Freak. I will never, ever forget or forgive her for drawing a moustache on my face at that sleepover in second grade. It was in permanent marker! I couldn't get it off for, like, two weeks!

HILLARY: I know. I saw it. And before you ask again, I was asleep when she did it, Geraldine. I swear that if I was awake, I'd never let her do that to you!

GERALD: She got Jackie Pomeranz to pull my gym shorts down in front of Matthew. So, OK, Jackie did it, but it was because of hideous Karen

Murray-Hoffman-Hinkley! She knew I liked Matthew. And she just pretended she didn't know anything about it. Please! I saw her laughing with Jackie before and after! She's guilty! There's no doubt in my mind. Karen Murray-Hoffman-Hickeyhead is evil, Hillary. We must crush her. I hate her buffalo butt and her troll face!

HILLARY: And she hates you, too, Geraldine!

GERALD: Let's curse her back!

HILLARY: Wait. We need to figure out what to do with you. Like what to call you and how you should act when we go out and what to tell people . . . We need to buy you all new clothes!

GERALD: Hold on. I think we're getting ahead of ourselves. Plus, I really do need to pee, Hill.

HILLARY: So go ahead already!

GERALD: I'm scared.

HILLARY: Come on. If boys can figure it out . . .

GERALD: OK. Good point.

HILLARY: Be brave.

GERALD: I'll try. Be back soon.

(GERALD *walks away.*)

HILLARY: Be brave, Ger!

Scene 2: The Transformation

HILLARY: Casey, I'm so worried. I think we've lost her.

CASEY: She does become more boyish every day.

HILLARY: I know! Yesterday instead of saying hi to me, she just nodded her head—like this!

(HILLARY demonstrates. She looks at CASEY and very slightly tilts her chin up, all the while looking very cool and unconcerned.)

CASEY: She did not!

HILLARY: She did! Not even a "hey" to go with it!

CASEY: We have to face it, Hill. She's gone.

HILLARY: She can't be gone! She's been my best friend since forever!

CASEY: We have to face facts. First of all, she's not a she. I mean, we know this, right?

HILLARY: Well, not first hand, but you should have seen her freak out the first time she—I mean he—had to go to the bathroom. If it wasn't so tragic, it would be funny.

CASEY: It sounds a little funny.

HILLARY: It was a little funny. But I couldn't laugh. You know.

CASEY: Of course.

HILLARY: But, see, that's just it. Girls are so concerned with others. We get people. We understand. Boys are clueless. And now that's how Geraldine is.

CASEY: Gerald.

HILLARY: I just cannot get used to calling her—

CASEY: him—

HILLARY: that.

CASEY: I know.

(GERALD, CARTER, and GRAHAM enter.)

CARTER: Hey.

GRAHAM: Hey.

(GERALD nods the same way HILLARY did at the top of the scene.)

HILLARY: (To CASEY.) See?

GERALD: What are you two doing here?

HILLARY: (Annoyed.) We were waiting for you. You said you'd meet us here an hour ago.

GERALD: Forgot.

CASEY: (Annoyed.) I guess so!

HILLARY: (Annoyed.) But we really enjoyed waiting for you.

GERALD: Oh. Good.

HILLARY: See? He doesn't get it.

CASEY: This is serious. He's gone over to the dark side.

GRAHAM: Are you talking about *Star Wars*?

HILLARY: No!

GRAHAM: Oh.

CASEY: So are we going to go now?

GERALD: Go where?

CASEY: The mall!

GERALD: Oh. I, uh, promised the guys I'd, um, play hockey.

HILLARY: No, you didn't!

CARTER: Sure he did.

HILLARY: He made that up just now because he didn't want to go to the mall with us. Very nice, Geraldine.

GERALD: Jeez, Hill! Don't call me that, OK? We've been through this, like, a million times!

HILLARY: Well, excuse me if I have a hard time calling you by your new name, Gerald. I've only been calling your Geraldine since kindergarten.

GERALD: Things change, babe.

CASEY: Did you just call her "babe"?

HILLARY: He did not call me "babe."

CASEY: He so called you "babe"!

HILLARY: You did not just call me "babe"!

GERALD: I called you "babe." Whatever! Girls are so dramatic.

CARTER: You can say that again.

GERALD: Girls are so dramatic.

CARTER: Good one, man.

HILLARY: So do you still like Matthew Flint, Gerald?

GERALD: No way! Shut up.

CARTER: You like Matthew Flint?

GERALD: No way. She's lost it.

GRAHAM: Girls.

GERALD: Girls.

HILLARY: I've had enough. Let's get out of here, Casey. We're wasted enough time with these Neanderthals.

CASEY: You said it!

(GRAHAM *starts making gorilla noises and movements. GERALD and CARTER join in.*)

HILLARY: Idiots!

(HILLARY and CASEY exit.)

GERALD: Finally!

GRAHAM: Hillary sure does follow you around.

GERALD: Whatever.

CARTER: Well, you were best friends.

GERALD: That was, like, another lifetime ago.

GRAHAM: Maybe she likes you.

GERALD: Dude, that's disgusting.

CARTER: She's not so bad. A little bossy . . .

GERALD: Like I said before, "Dude, that's disgusting."

CARTER: So . . . what if . . .

(Beat.)

GRAHAM: What if what?

CARTER: What if I asked her out?

GRAHAM: You'd do that?

CARTER: Maybe.

GRAHAM: Seriously?

CARTER: I don't know. Maybe. I haven't exactly decided.

GERALD: Whatever.

CARTER: You mean it?

GERALD: It's not like I like her.

GRAHAM: But you do like girls, right?

GERALD: I'm a guy, Graham.

GRAHAM: Right, just checking.

CARTER: But you must know a lot about girls, having been one once.

GERALD: Listen, I don't really want to talk about it. One day I just woke up and I was a guy. It was, like, magic or something. And since then, I sort of forgot all about what stuff was like before. I don't know anything about girls, Carter.

CARTER: You must remember some stuff.

GRAHAM: You had big boo—

GERALD: Shut up or I will kill you, Graham. I mean it.

GRAHAM: Calm down, man. We just never . . . you know. So we're curious.

CARTER: But if you don't want to talk about it—

GERALD: I don't want to talk about it. That's one thing

I know that's different. I don't want to talk about anything ever again. That's girl stuff.

CARTER: Cool.

GRAHAM: Why do girls like shopping? It's boring. And what about shows where people cry? If I see one person cry, I'm turning off the TV. No question. And shoes! All shoes look the same. I mean, some are different colors, I guess, but so what? Can you imagine having a baby? That is so wrong! I don't even want to think about it!

CARTER: Girls think sports and video games are boring.

GRAHAM: Why do girls think sports and video games are boring? In what universe are those things boring? That's sick. Sick! Girls sit around talking and thinking and thinking and talking and shopping and talking, but they don't get anything. If I had to live like that, with no fun, I don't know what I'd do. Plus, I don't ever want to do laundry. Being a girl is the pits. I'm so glad I'm a guy. We make sense at least.

GERALD: For a guy, you're talking a lot right now.

GRAHAM: I don't talk too much! I'm done talking now. I probably won't talk again for the next twenty years.

(Beat. HILLARY and CASEY enter suddenly.)

HILLARY: OK. We're going to change you back.

GRAHAM: Are you going to do surgery or something?

CARTER: I saw that once on TV. It was sick.

GRAHAM: That's gross. Why did you watch?

CARTER: I don't know. Because it was gross, I guess.

HILLARY: Shut up.

CARTER: So, Hillary, I was wondering—

HILLARY: Shut up, Carter!

CARTER: OK.

GRAHAM: Burn! She got you, man!

HILLARY: Which part of shut up don't you get, Graham?

GRAHAM: None of—

HILLARY: Shut. Up. So, Gerald, we went to Casey's house. She has three brothers.

CASEY: Each one more dirty and slobby than the last.

HILLARY: And we raided the house.

CASEY: We had to wear dishwashing gloves because we didn't want to touch anything.

HILLARY: And we brought back a few items to show you.

GERALD: That's nice. So, we're going to play hockey—

HILLARY: Stay right where you are. Casey? Item One.

(CASEY puts on plastic gloves, goes into a plastic bag, and pulls out a sock.)

CASEY: Here, Gerald.

(GERALD takes the sock. HILLARY and CASEY pinch their noses.)

GERALD: It's a sock.

CASEY: This is not just an ordinary sock. This is a smelly sock worn by my brother, John, during baseball practice. His feet are sweaty, and he's probably worn them about thirty times without washing them. If there is any girliness left in you, this will bring it out.

HILLARY: Smell it.

(GERALD smells the sock.)

GERALD: Yeah. It smells.

HILLARY: That's it?

CASEY: I swear, I thought I was going to die when John took off his sneakers yesterday and he was wearing those socks! Really! I thought I was actually going to die. I don't know how you guys can stand to even be in the same room with socks like these.

GRAHAM: Jeez, it's just a sock.

CARTER: I've got lots of socks like this one.

CASEY: I really don't understand boys! How does filth not bother you? Are you faking it to look cool? Are you really secretly disgusted?

GRAHAM: Nope.

CASEY: I admit it. Men are a complete mystery. I don't know how I'm ever going to marry one of you.

GERALD: Good, 'cause none of us are interested.

CASEY: I meant as an entire sex, not just you guys.

CARTER: She said "sex"!

CASEY: I give up. I mean it. I'm going to become a nun.

HILLARY: OK. This is going to take more drastic measures, Casey. Take out Item Two.

(CASEY takes out a bowl.)

CASEY: This, we think, used to be meatballs. We can't be entirely sure. I would date this . . . substance . . . back about two months. I think my mom's afraid to touch it. I saw it move once.

GERALD: That's not an ordinary meatball. That's a meatball sandwich deluxe.

CASEY: What?

GERALD: A meatball deluxe. I made one last week. It's meatballs with Doritos and potato chips smashed into it, put on top of bread with peanut butter, and chili on top to make the bread mushy.

CARTER: Awesome!

CASEY: I'm going to be sick. I think I gotta go home now, Hillary.

HILLARY: Fine. I understand. Thanks, Casey.

(CASEY exits.)

HILLARY: Well, I guess that's it, Gerald. You're a completely different person. You probably like Karen Murray-Hoffman-Hinkley now.

GERALD: I'm not that different.

HILLARY: Well, that's a relief.

GERALD: I just think we can't be best friends anymore. I'm not the same. Plus . . . you just . . . know too much about me before. And I can't be that person anymore.

(HILLARY is quiet.)

GERALD: You're mad.

HILLARY: No.

GERALD: Sad?

HILLARY: No. I understand. It's OK. I'll just miss you, Geraldi—Gerald. You know what I mean.

GERALD: Yeah.

HILLARY: So. I guess I'll go home.

GERALD: OK.

(HILLARY leaves. Beat.)

CARTER: So . . . I got a new game yesterday. I've got it with me.

GRAHAM: Video game?

CARTER: Yeah.

GERALD: I'm going to beat both of you.

GRAHAM: I'm playing first!

CARTER: No way!

(GRAHAM and CARTER race out of the room. GERALD waits for a beat, then quickly throws out the sock and the bowl.)

GERALD: Nasty!

TALK BACK!

1. What makes boys different from girls personality-wise?

2. What are some stereotypes about boys/girls? Is there any truth to these stereotypes? Are they fair?

3. What's the first thing you'd do if you could switch genders?

4. What don't you understand about the opposite sex?

5. Have you ever grown apart from a friend?

6. Have you ever been mean to a friend to get some distance from him or her? Why?

7. What do you think Gerald will be like in the future?

8. Do you think Gerald would be accepted at your school? Why or why not?

9. Imitating the opposite gender's behavior can be great fun. However, there are also common pitfalls. Girls, what do boys do when imitating you that's not realistic? Boys, what do girls do when they're imitating you that's not realistic?

THE PLOT THICKENS

5F, 2M

WHO

    FEMALES   MALES
      Allegra   Holden
      Ann   Marius
      Lana
      Nancy
      Tuesday

WHERE The school auditorium.

WHEN Present day.

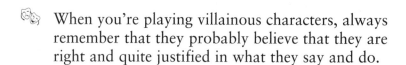 When you're playing villainous characters, always remember that they probably believe that they are right and quite justified in what they say and do.

Write a play where your main characters are villains.

Scene 1: Chicken Soup

(ALLEGRA is sweeping the stage.)

ALLEGRA: *(Grandly.)* Me! Sweeping the stage? And why? Because they think I'm not good enough. What do they know? Nothing! The fools. Can't they see my genius? I'm clearly vastly superior to that sorry excuse for a leading lady. They're all jealous. Jealous! But they'll be sorry. I'll make them sorry. They will pay for snubbing me. No one treats me poorly and gets away with it. I will not be ignored! This is not the life I was meant to lead. I was born to be a star—going to premieres, smiling for the camera, waving at my loyal fans. This is beneath me! I have dignity, dammit. And I will not be brought low by small-minded, small-town bumpkins. Little will they suspect the misery that awaits. My acting talents will be on full display; they will not even guess! But they will rue the day they asked me to sweep the stage. THEY WILL RUE THE DAY, I TELL YOU!

(Applause is heard from backstage. TUESDAY enters.)

TUESDAY: That was excellent, Allegra.

ALLEGRA: Thanks, Tuesday. Just going over my lines.

TUESDAY: You're going to be amazing.

ALLEGRA: Thanks! You, too.

TUESDAY: Well, I'm only the Messenger.

ALLEGRA: But you deliver that message really well.

TUESDAY: Do you think so?

ALLEGRA: Oh, definitely. You'll get a better part next year for sure.

TUESDAY: But I'll never be as good as you.

ALLEGRA: Well, my acting coach says I have natural talent. You know, the It factor.

TUESDAY: Oh, yeah, completely. I mean, you've gotten the lead for three shows in a row. That's, like, a record.

ALLEGRA: I work hard, though. I don't want to let anyone down.

TUESDAY: As if you could.

ALLEGRA: You're so sweet!

TUESDAY: Thanks!

ALLEGRA: Well, I've got to go. By the way, this stage is filthy. Who's really supposed to sweep it?

TUESDAY: I don't know. I'll find out.

ALLEGRA: You're a doll.

(ALLEGRA exits.)

TUESDAY: Holden?

(HOLDEN enters.)

HOLDEN: Yep?

TUESDAY: Allegra asked me to ask you who's supposed to sweep the stage. It's dirty.

HOLDEN: That would be Nancy.

TUESDAY: Well, could you tell her to do it? Allegra was a little upset.

HOLDEN: Isn't she supposed to sweep the stage in that one scene anyway?

TUESDAY: So?

HOLDEN: So it's more realistic if it's dirty anyway.

TUESDAY: Holden! She was really upset. A person could, I don't know, slip or something if the stage is dirty.

HOLDEN: I was just kidding, OK? Take it easy. What are you, her assistant or something?

TUESDAY: She just asked me to find out who needs to sweep the stage, that's all.

HOLDEN: What is it about Allegra that makes people do what she wants?

TUESDAY: She's sweet.

HOLDEN: If you say so.

TUESDAY: I do. So will you see that it gets done? The floors? I mean, you're the stage manager so Nancy's supposed to do what you say, right?

HOLDEN: That's the theory.

TUESDAY: So, are you going to do it?

HOLDEN: Yeah, yeah. Just take it easy.

(TUESDAY exits.)

HOLDEN: Nancy? Nancy!

(NANCY enters.)

NANCY: Did you call me?

HOLDEN: Yeah, Nance, sweep and mop the stage.

NANCY: What?

HOLDEN: You're my assistant and I'm asking you to assist.

NANCY: Yeah, but isn't that the janitor's job?

HOLDEN: Are you refusing?

NANCY: Well, no, but—

HOLDEN: I only want to work with team players.

NANCY: But cleaning the floor?

HOLDEN: That's what needs to be done.

NANCY: What are you going to be doing?

HOLDEN: I need a coffee.

NANCY: Where are you going to get coffee?

HOLDEN: I'm going to go to Starbucks.

NANCY: Could I get one?

HOLDEN: Sure. If you sweep and mop the stage like I asked you to.

NANCY: But isn't Allegra already sweeping the stage in the play?

HOLDEN: It still needs to be clean. Now, sweep it first, then mop it.

(HOLDEN starts to leave.)

NANCY: Wait!

HOLDEN: What is it now?

NANCY: My order. You don't know what I want.

HOLDEN: OK, fine. You'd better give me money, though.

NANCY: No problem. I want a grande latte with vanilla, OK?

HOLDEN: Sure. Give me the money.

(NANCY gives HOLDEN some money.)

NANCY: You'll remember, right?

HOLDEN: I'll try.

(HOLDEN exits. NANCY picks up the broom.)

NANCY: Doesn't seem fair that I should have to sweep the stage while he gets coffee. None of this seems fair. *(Beat.)* Me! Sweeping the stage. And why? Because they think I'm not good enough. What do they know? Nothing! The fools. Can't they see my genius? I'm clearly vastly superior to that sorry excuse for a leading lady. They're all jealous. Jealous! But they'll be sorry. I'll make them sorry. They will pay for snubbing me. No one treats me poorly and gets away with it. I will not be ignored! This is not the life I was meant to lead. I was born to be a star—going to premieres, smiling for the camera, waving at my loyal fans. This is beneath me! I have dignity, dammit. And I will not be brought low by small-minded, small-town bumpkins. Little will they suspect the misery that awaits. My acting talents will be on full display; they will not even guess! But they will rue the day they asked me to sweep the stage. THEY WILL RUE THE DAY, I TELL YOU!

(LANA enters.)

LANA: What are you doing?

NANCY: Um, I was just sweeping the stage.

LANA: You were saying Allegra's lines. Badly.

NANCY: Thanks.

LANA: You don't think you're an actress, do you?

NANCY: I could be if I wanted to.

LANA: No, you couldn't. You're a techie. Those two things do not mix.

NANCY: If you know everything, then why are you playing the mother?

LANA: The mother is a very fine role. I have a lot of lines. I'm a very important character.

NANCY: A very important *old* character.

LANA: At least I can act. At least I can get a part in the first place! I believe you auditioned and did not even get a measly chorus role. You must have really stunk. In fact, I remember Holden saying that your audition was actually funny. Not on purpose, though. What was your audition piece?

NANCY: It was Shakespeare. Juliet.

LANA: Ah, yes. Juliet. I remember now. He said that it was grotesque, you acting like you were in love and roaming around awkwardly trying to look dreamy-eyed. He said it was embarrassing to watch.

NANCY: Holden is a stage manager, not an actor. What does he know?

LANA: Holden knows a lot more than you. If you're going to be an actress, techie, you're going to need to learn how to take constructive criticism. It's important to becoming a better actor. I'm just trying to help you. You might want to try less . . . romantic roles. It's not exactly believable to think that some guy would kill himself to be with you. But it would save you a lot of misery if you just faced that you're not cut out for this. *(Beat.)* You look upset. Poor thing. But it's better that you learn now that you don't have it. I don't want you to embarrass yourself again.

NANCY: You're very generous.

LANA: Just trying to help. Oh, you missed a spot.

NANCY: I just started.

LANA: Oh. Well. You'd better get to work then. Holden's going to be back with our pizza any moment now.

NANCY: Pizza?

LANA: It's for the two of us. Don't get too excited.

(LANA exits.)

NANCY: All I have is a cup of chicken noodle soup.

(HOLDEN enters.)

HOLDEN: Did you see Lana? I've got our pizza and coffee.

NANCY: Where's mine?

HOLDEN: What?

NANCY: My latte?

HOLDEN: Oh. Forgot.

NANCY: Nice. Well, can I have my money back then?

HOLDEN: Sorry. I used it to pay for the pizza. Can I pay you back tomorrow?

NANCY: Can I have some pizza?

HOLDEN: There's just enough for two.

NANCY: But I paid for it.

HOLDEN: But I promised Lana. I'll pay you back tomorrow. Hey—you missed a spot. I thought you'd be done by now! Hurry up and clean the stage already, Nancy! Time is money!

(HOLDEN exits.)

NANCY: Me! Sweeping the stage. And why? Because they think I'm not good enough. What do they know? Nothing! The fools . . . But they will rue the day they asked me to sweep the stage. They will rue the day.

Scene 2: Clam Chowder

ALLEGRA: *(Dramatically.)* I will love you always!

(ALLEGRA and MARIUS move closer, as if to kiss. MARIUS pulls away quickly.)

MARIUS: Um, could we take a break?

(HOLDEN enters.)

HOLDEN: OK, people, let's take ten.

ALLEGRA: And it was just getting good, Marius!

MARIUS: Right. Sorry.

(ALLEGRA exits.)

MARIUS: Holden!

HOLDEN: What?

MARIUS: Can I talk to you for a minute?

HOLDEN: Sure. But I'm really busy.

MARIUS: It won't take long.

(HOLDEN walks over to MARIUS.)

HOLDEN: What is it?

MARIUS: It's Allegra.

HOLDEN: What about her?

MARIUS: It's just that . . . I don't want to be unprofessional or a complainer or anything, but . . .

HOLDEN: What is it?

MARIUS: She . . . smells. I didn't want to say anything, but . . .

HOLDEN: What is it? Her breath? 'Cause we can give her a mint.

MARIUS: No, it's worse.

HOLDEN: I never noticed that she smelled before.

MARIUS: Neither did I! But today . . . it's really bad. She reeks. I didn't want to tell her in case it hurt her feelings or something.

HOLDEN: Right.

MARIUS: I didn't want it to affect our work, you know? It would be terrible for our onstage chemistry if Allegra thought I said something bad about her. Especially that she smells. I mean, that's really kind of a rude thing to say. But it's true, Holden. I'm serious. I'm not just saying this. It's for real. *(Beat.)* I know it's not exactly fair of me to ask you to do this, but would you tell her? I wouldn't ask if it wasn't completely necessary. I nearly puked on her a minute ago.

HOLDEN: I thought you were into Allegra. I was wondering why you didn't kiss her.

MARIUS: I do like Allegra. I did, anyway. She's really cool and she's pretty and, before today, I would not have minded kissing her. But now . . . I just can't be with a girl who smells like sewage. I don't think it's too much to ask for someone to smell clean. Soap is not that hard to come by. I just think it's professional to not smell when you have to be in a play and you're forced to stand close to someone. I think that's a reasonable request.

HOLDEN: OK. I'll talk to her.

MARIUS: Don't say it came from me, though. OK?

HOLDEN: Sure.

MARIUS: Thanks.

(MARIUS exits.)

HOLDEN: Allegra? Is Allegra around here?

(ALLEGRA enters.)

ALLEGRA: You called?

HOLDEN: Yeah, Allegra. Can you come over here for a sec?

ALLEGRA: If I must. I'd prefer to be on break though.

HOLDEN: It's just for a sec.

ALLEGRA: Fine.

(ALLEGRA walks over to HOLDEN.)

HOLDEN: OK. It seems that someone said that—Whoa!

(HOLDEN steps away from ALLEGRA.)

ALLEGRA: What?

HOLDEN: Whoa.

ALLEGRA: What? I have to go practice my lines, Holden. I don't have time for games.

HOLDEN: It's just that . . . wow. You really smell.

ALLEGRA: Excuse me?

HOLDEN: You smell horrible.

ALLEGRA: Very funny. I do not. What you're smelling is an expensive perfume called Tryst. You either have terrible taste or this is a lame joke that's wasting my time.

HOLDEN: I am being completely serious. You need to take a shower.

ALLEGRA: I'm perfectly clean.

(ALLEGRA starts to walk away.)

HOLDEN: That's why Marius didn't want to kiss you.

ALLEGRA: What?

HOLDEN: I can hardly blame him. I can't believe he lasted as long as he did.

ALLEGRA: But . . . it's not me! It can't be me.

HOLDEN: It's you.

ALLEGRA: Lana?

(TUESDAY enters.)

TUESDAY: Did you call me?

ALLEGRA: No, but you'll do. Come here.

(TUESDAY walks quickly over to ALLEGRA. When she reaches ALLEGRA, TUESDAY tries to subtly back away and turn her face from the stench.)

ALLEGRA: Do I smell?

TUESDAY: Um . . .

ALLEGRA: Do I smell?

TUESDAY: Well . . .

(LANA enters.)

LANA: What do you want, Allegra?

ALLEGRA: Good, Lana. Tell me . . . *(Quieter.)* Come here and tell me if I smell.

(LANA walks over.)

LANA: Whoa! You smell awful. Like rancid clam chowder.

ALLEGRA: Did I smell earlier today?

LANA: No. You smelled like Tryst.

ALLEGRA: So it must be . . . this dress! This costume!

HOLDEN: Well, please, put on another.

ALLEGRA: I don't have another that's appropriate for this scene.

HOLDEN: Then put on your regular clothes.

(ALLEGRA exits. TUESDAY follows. HOLDEN watches them exit. At the same time, LANA starts scratching madly.)

HOLDEN: Boy, that costume was nast—

(LANA is scratching her butt.)

HOLDEN: Lana?

LANA: Oh! What?

HOLDEN: Were you just . . . scratching your butt?

LANA: No, I was just . . . I thought I sat in something.

HOLDEN: So . . . But you were scratching your butt.

LANA: No, I wasn't.

HOLDEN: OK. Whatever.

(HOLDEN turns away, and LANA goes back to madly scratching. HOLDEN turns back quickly and catches her again.)

HOLDEN: Ha! You are scratching your butt!

LANA: No! It's just . . .

HOLDEN: Just what?

LANA: I don't know.

HOLDEN: Do you have a problem or something?

LANA: No! Don't be stupid.

HOLDEN: Just checking. 'Cause if you've got a problem you could go to the nurse or something.

LANA: I don't have a problem.

(LANA is trying desperately not to scratch, but she really, really wants to.)

HOLDEN: Are you sure?

LANA: Yes! Yes!

HOLDEN: You didn't fall into some poison ivy during gym class or anything?

LANA: Please. I'm fine. So you can just—go away!

(HOLDEN exits as MARIUS enters. LANA starts scratching fiercely again.)

MARIUS: Um, hi.

(LANA turns and sees MARIUS.)

LANA: Poison ivy.

MARIUS: OK.

(LANA runs off. MARIUS exits. ANN and NANCY enter.)

NANCY: Told you.

ANN: Brilliant.

NANCY: You haven't seen anything yet.

ANN: But don't you feel bad? I mean, they are human beings still. It's good to see Allegra and Lana embarrassed, but it also reminds me that they're human, too. They both got humiliated in front of the guys they like. That's the worst. I can tell you that from experience. In sixth grade, I thought I was so cool and I went to a dance and busted into this dance move in front of Justin Avery. I seriously thought it was so cool. The look on his face— it was like Medusa appeared before him. He just sort of stared with these huge eyes and his mouth hanging open like he was seeing this hideous beast. Which I guess must have been how I looked. To this day, Justin Avery walks a big circle around me whenever he sees me in the hall. Before that dance, I really thought he liked me, too. I still wonder about that. So it makes me wonder whether this revenge is exactly fair.

NANCY: Of course it's fair. Allegra and Lana need to be taken down. So does Holden. He's rude. If they were nice people, I wouldn't mind that they got parts in the play and I didn't. I wouldn't mind that Holden tells me what to do if he would only be a little bit polite about it. But they're all so smug and horrible about it. So my next move will be—

ANN: I don't know if I want to know!

NANCY: Then wait and see.

TALK BACK!

1. Does Allegra deserve her punishment? Why or why not?

2. Revenge is sweet. True or false?

3. What do you think happens next?

4. What do you think would be the "adult" way for Nancy to handle Lana, Allegra, and Holden? Is that what you would do? Why or why not?

5. Being passive aggressive means taking aggressive action in a secretive, indirect way. Nancy's actions are passive aggressive. What have you done that's passive aggressive?

6. Do you think you see yourself realistically or do you have an idealized vision of yourself? Do you think your view of yourself should be more positive or more critical?

SPACE SWITCH

4F, 4M

WHO

FEMALES	MALES
Edina	Bill
Lauren	Bob
Lily	Phil
Lucy	Sebastian

WHERE Scene 1: Edina's bedroom; Scene 2: Phil's bedroom.

WHEN Present day.

🎭 See if you can "pick up your cues": Say your line *just* after the previous line is spoken. You need to be sure you don't hurry your lines, it's not a race, but don't leave long pauses between your lines. It keeps the energy going and the scene moving forward.

✎ You're left alone with a favorite object (a diary, a piece of clothing, etc.) of a friend or a sibling. You can do the right thing or you can do the wrong thing. Write two scenes exploring each option and its aftermath.

Scene 1: Challenged

SEBASTIAN: Why did you think this would be a good idea?

PHIL: She thought she could do this better than us. As if.

SEBASTIAN: Do we want to do a better job than them?

PHIL: What do you mean?

SEBASTIAN: I mean it would be funny to do a really terrible job. Like give her a neon yellow room.

PHIL: But she's going to be doing my room.

SEBASTIAN: So?

PHIL: So, I don't want her taking revenge.

SEBASTIAN: She won't know.

PHIL: Sure she will.

SEBASTIAN: Not 'til it's over.

PHIL: True . . .

SEBASTIAN: So we do an ugly room then.

PHIL: Yeah, but then she's still be able to say that guys have no sense and we're stupid and we're all color blind.

SEBASTIAN: So what? And you'll be able to laugh and

laugh at the thought of her trying to sleep in her neon yellow room.

(LAUREN and BOB enter. BOB is filming.)

LAUREN: Hi, guys! Welcome to *Switching Spaces*, the only decorating show on television where kids do everything! I'm your designer, Lauren. So do you know what you want to do with this room?

SEBASTIAN: We were thinking neon.

PHIL: No we weren't!

LAUREN: You weren't? What were you thinking then?

PHIL: We were thinking . . .

SEBASTIAN: Neon!

PHIL: No, Sebastian!

LAUREN: Well, what does Edina like, guys?

PHIL: She likes . . . fruit.

LAUREN: Fruit.

PHIL: Yeah. She really likes oranges.

LAUREN: I have got the greatest idea. We can combine your ideas! We'll do neon fruit!

SEBASTIAN: Yeah! Excellent!

PHIL: I'm not sure she'll—

LAUREN: It's going to be fantastic, right? I can't wait to start. So why don't we just start getting to it?

BOB: OK, cut.

(BOB exits.)

LAUREN: I'm going to go get some neon paint now. This room will be electric!

PHIL: Yeah, about that—

SEBASTIAN: Don't be a wimp, Phil.

LAUREN: What's the problem, Phil?

PHIL: I don't really know that this theme is such a good idea.

LAUREN: Why? It'll be fun!

PHIL: Well, it doesn't sound very . . . nice.

LAUREN: Please, Phil. I'm a professional. I know what's nice. I've designed for lots of these shows.

SEBASTIAN: Phil, don't be such a wimp.

LAUREN: Is it the color scheme?

PHIL: Yeah. Neon's not so good. It's not very . . . peaceful.

LAUREN: It's active. Lively. **Many people are afraid of color, Phil. But that's why I'm here. I'm going to help you. Everything's going to be OK. We'll get** through this together. Let me show you some color samples.

(LAUREN *takes out some brightly colored pieces of paper.*)

LAUREN: What do you think of this?

PHIL: It's really, really pink.

LAUREN: That's right, Phil. It is pink. And how does pink make you feel?

PHIL: Um, horrible.

LAUREN: Aw. You don't need to be afraid of pink, Phil. Pink isn't out to get you. It's your friend. Touch the pink, Phil. Touch it.

PHIL: I don't need to touch—

LAUREN: *(Very firmly, dropping her perky façade.)* Touch it, Phil. I don't have all day.

(*Intimidated,* PHIL *touches the pink paper.*)

LAUREN: Was that so bad? I can tell from your face that it wasn't. See? Color is good. Color is healthy, Phil. People need color. Edina needs color. It will brighten her life. And the sooner you get over your fear, the better. Because I am going to paint these walls neon pink with bright yellow bananas stenciled everywhere. And it's going to be fabulous, Phil. Fabulous! Say it with me, Phil. Fabulous! *(Beat.)* I *said* say it with me, Phil.

PHIL/LAUREN: **Fabulous!**

LAUREN: **That's right, Phil. Don't you forget it.** Well, I feel better now. I don't know about you.

PHIL: I feel better! I feel better! Just no more, please!

LAUREN: Rest up, boys. We're going to be painting soon!

(LAUREN exits. BOB enters.)

BOB: Uh, guys? **First of all, was it a dare or something?**

SEBASTIAN: What?

BOB: **The reason you're doing this.**

PHIL: Sort of.

BOB: **It's always a dare or really wanting to be on TV. Occasionally, someone is actually interested in decorating for some reason. And then other times, it's revenge against either the person whose room you're decorating or your parents. Parents always hate the rooms because they nail and staple things to the wall and basically destroy your house.**

PHIL: Are you serious? They're in my house now!

BOB: I know, I know. **You guys seem pretty cool, so I just wanted to give you a heads up. Unless you really hate this girl whose room you're doing, do not let them talk you into anything. I have seen many friendships ruined because of this show. I have seen people become mortal enemies. One time in Delaware, a guy lost his eye. I'm serious. The kid** said the girl really liked cows because one time she said that cows were cute. So they painted cow spots on the walls and made her bed look like a cow and put udders under her desk. The girl takes one look at the room and is like, "Are you saying I'm a cow?" And before you know it, pop! There goes the kid's eye. Don't let them talk you into anything. Your room might be awful to look at when they're done, but at least you'll still be able to see.

(BOB exits.)

PHIL: Sebastian, did you hear that?

SEBASTIAN: I'm standing right here.

PHIL: We have to stop that Lauren girl before she buys that paint!

SEBASTIAN: Too late. She's gone. Besides, I'm scared of her.

PHIL: Well, me too, but I don't want Edina to kill me when she sees her neon fruity room!

SEBASTIAN: She won't kill you.

PHIL: She might.

SEBASTIAN: She won't! Chill! There won't be any cows on the walls. What will she have to complain about?

PHIL: Who knows! She's a girl. She could complain that I think she's fruity or that she's shaped like an apple—who knows! Like girls need a logical reason to be mad. I have two sisters and a mother and don't understand anything about women. We need this room to be white or something! Plain. Nothing at all.

SEBASTIAN: You don't think that will make her mad, too?

PHIL: I don't know what to do. This is a huge mistake. Why did I agree to this?

SEBASTIAN: Pride.

PHIL: Oh, right.

(LAUREN reenters with BOB.)

LAUREN: This is going to be so fun. Then over the desk we're going to write, "You're grape." Isn't that cute? Are you getting this Bob?

PHIL: We are so dead.

SEBASTIAN: If Edina doesn't kill us, the kids at school will.

Scene 2: Talent

EDINA: I've always wanted to be on TV.

LILY: Not me. I really don't want to do this, Edina.

EDINA: Don't be shy, Lily. I'll do all the talking if you don't want to.

LILY: I don't want to be on TV at all, Edina. Talking has nothing to do with it. Can't you find someone else?

EDINA: No, I can't find someone else. I want you to help me with this.

LILY: Why?

EDINA: Because.

LILY: Fine. But I'm not saying anything!

(LUCY enters with BILL, the cameraman.)

LUCY: Hi, gang! Welcome to *Switching Spaces*, the only decorating show on television where kids do everything! I'm your designer, Lucy. Do you have any decorating ideas?

EDINA: I was thinking "Room on Mars" as our theme. Lots of fiery reds and a working volcano.

LUCY: Excellent! And we could put thick foam all over the floor so it will be like you're bouncing around in zero gravity.

EDINA: Cool!

LILY: Won't it be hard to get around?

LUCY: No. It will be great!

EDINA: We could paint little green aliens on the walls, too.

LUCY: Perfect!

LILY: But will you be able to open the closet door if there's foam on the floor?

LUCY: We'll shorten the closet door.

EDINA: It should look like slime is hanging from the ceiling.

LILY: Why?

EDINA: Everyone knows Mars is slimy.

LILY: It is?

LUCY: It is now! Let's get to work, girls!

LILY: I don't know about this.

LUCY: OK, cut, Bill.

(BILL exits.)

LUCY: **Listen, you need to get on board here. We're a team and you're not acting like a team player.**

LILY: I was just bringing up some points that seemed important.

LUCY: Who is the designer here?

LILY: Well, you.

LUCY: That's right! Me! And that means you do what I say, got it? If I say we're creating an enormous hole in the wall, we're doing it.

EDINA: Sounds good!

LUCY: If I say we're lighting old tires on fire and attaching them to the wall, we're doing it.

EDINA: He'll love that!

LUCY: If I say we're making an art project with sausages and Post-It notes, we're doing it!

EDINA: Are the sausages cooked?

LUCY: We're doing it! We're doing all of it! And it will be brilliant. Everyone will want to do it. People on the streets will say, "My God, I need to have some sausages on my wall, too! If my room doesn't look just like that, I do not know how I will go on."

LILY: But people don't talk like that.

LUCY: Kid, are you in or out? Because I can call a casting agent and get this girl another best friend in five minutes flat if I need to. What's it going to be?

LILY: Edina, maybe you should get someone else to help. I don't know if I can do this.

(LUCY pulls out a phone.)

LUCY: Hey, Bernie! Listen, I'm here doing this decorating show even though I'd rather be doing that film role you promised me—I could easily play a fifty-year-old bus driver who's husband left her to make mannequins in New York so she has to rebuild her life with her six children! I am not too young, Bernie! Anyway, I need a kid here, pronto. A best friend. Someone chatty and agreeable. And cute. But not too cute! Not cuter than me. Yeah, we've got a really difficult one here now. And I just don't have time for this. I have a career to save here. It's bad enough you don't get me any decent work. The least you can do is get me some decent people to work with. This one is a real dead fish. I don't need to deal with this sort of thing, Bernie. I'm getting very upset. You don't know how vulnerable I am. Do you know that I can cry on cue? I'm about to do that right now because this job is really stinking, Bernie. I've got this loudmouthed kid here—Help me out here, Bernie!

LILY: I was just speaking my mind! I didn't mean to be difficult.

EDINA: Please don't go, Lily. Please! I want you to be here to help me!

LILY: But I don't know if I agree . . . I don't know if I want to be responsible in case Phil doesn't like it.

EDINA: Lily, he's going to blame me if he doesn't like it, not you. But it's going to have a working volcano! It sounds perfect for him!

LILY: That does sound good. But I don't know about the rest.

EDINA: Please, Lily. Do it for me.

LUCY: Hold on, Bernie. It's just some kids talking. What? Are you sure? The difficult one? OK, I guess.

(LUCY holds the phone out to LILY.)

LUCY: He says he wants to talk to you.

(LILY takes the phone.)

LILY: Hello? . . . I'm Lily . . . Well, I don't know . . . I never thought . . . But I'm not . . . Are you sure? . . . I'm only . . . I've never been the kind of person . . . Well . . . OK.

(LILY hands the phone back to LUCY.)

LUCY: Hello? Bernie?

LILY: He hung up.

LUCY: Oh.

LILY: Edina, he's sending another best friend over here for you. Apparently, I'm not right for this show.

EDINA: Oh, Lily. I'm so sorry!

LILY: It's OK.

LUCY: Better luck next time.

LILY: Well, I've got to go. A limo's going to be picking me up.

LUCY: A limo?

EDINA: How come?

LILY: It seems I just got the role of a fifty-year-old truck driver whose husband left her to become a mannequin maker in New York City. Now she has to raise her six kids alone. It sounds like a very sad story.

LUCY: That's my role!

LILY: He said they needed someone with values and strong convictions.

LUCY: I have convictions!

LILY: I don't know. I'm just saying what he said.

EDINA: But I'm the one who wants to be on TV, not you!

LILY: You will be on TV.

EDINA: But I wanted to be in a movie, too! Why should you get it? You don't even want it!

LILY: I know. I tried to tell him, but he wouldn't listen.

LUCY: You're too young for that role!

LILY: He said they'd use makeup.

LUCY: That was my idea!

EDINA: This is so unfair! The one thing I've always dreamed of, always wanted, and you're the one getting it!

(BILL enters.)

BILL: There's a limo here for Lily?

LILY: OK. Thanks. Well, I'm sorry, Edina. I really am. But I just know this show is going to go great for you. And this room will be just . . . so interesting when you're done.

(LILY exits. PHIL rushes in.)

PHIL: Edina, we have to talk about this. I don't know if this is a good idea.

EDINA: You're not supposed to be in here!

PHIL: I know, but I think this whole thing is a mistake.

LUCY: Not another downer.

EDINA: What are you saying, Phil?

PHIL: Let's just forget the whole thing.

EDINA: The TV show?

PHIL: Yeah.

EDINA: The whole, *whole* thing?

PHIL: Yeah!

EDINA: So I will never, ever be on TV?

PHIL: I guess so.

EDINA: And you think that's a good idea?

PHIL: Definitely!

EDINA: Thanks a lot!

(EDINA launches herself at PHIL, as if to attack him.)

PHIL: No! Not the eyes! My face! My beautiful face! Please, Edina! Have I ever told you you're grape?

EDINA: You're an idiot, Phil!

(BOB enters. BILL pulls out his camera.)

BOB: Not again!

BILL: It makes great television . . .

TALK BACK!

1. If you could be on one TV show, which one would it be and why?

2. If you had to redecorate a friend's room, would you try to do a good job or would you mess it up as a joke? Be specific about what you'd do and why.

3. Would you find being on national TV fun or embarrassing? Why?

4. Are you a leader or a follower? Do you like to give orders or let others make the big decisions? Why?

5. If you could have your room any way you wanted, what would you do and why?

APPENDIX

CHARACTER QUESTIONNAIRE FOR ACTORS

Fill in the following questionnaire as if you are your character. Make up anything you don't know.

PART 1: The Facts

NAME:

AGE/BIRTHDATE:

HEIGHT:

WEIGHT:

HAIR COLOR:

EYE COLOR:

CITY/STATE/COUNTRY YOU LIVE IN:

GRADE*:

BROTHERS/SISTERS:

PARENTS:

UPBRINGING (strict, indifferent, permissive, etc.):

---

* If you are an adult, what educational level did you reach (college, medical school, high school, etc.)?

PART 2: Rate Yourself

On a scale of 1 to 10 (circle one: 10 = great, 1 = bad), rate your:

APPEARANCE	1 2 3 4 5 6 7 8 9 10
IQ	1 2 3 4 5 6 7 8 9 10
SENSE OF HUMOR	1 2 3 4 5 6 7 8 9 10
ATHLETICISM	1 2 3 4 5 6 7 8 9 10
ENTHUSIASM	1 2 3 4 5 6 7 8 9 10
CONFIDENCE	1 2 3 4 5 6 7 8 9 10
DETERMINATION	1 2 3 4 5 6 7 8 9 10
FRIENDLINESS	1 2 3 4 5 6 7 8 9 10
ARTISTICNESS	1 2 3 4 5 6 7 8 9 10

Do you like yourself?	YES	NO
Do you like your family?	YES	NO
Do you like the opposite sex?	YES	NO
Do you like most people you meet?	YES	NO

Which of the following are important to you and which are not?
Circle one.

WEALTH	Important	Not Important
KNOWLEDGE	Important	Not Important
POWER	Important	Not Important
PEACE	Important	Not Important
POPULARITY	Important	Not Important
LIKABILITY	Important	Not Important
LOVE	Important	Not Important
SPIRITUALITY/RELIGION	Important	Not Important

PART 3: Favorites

List your favorites (be specific).

FOOD:

SONG:

BOOK:

MOVIE:

TV SHOW:

CITY:

SEASON:

COLOR:

PIECE OF CLOTHING:

SMELL:

ANIMAL:

SOUND:

SCHOOL SUBJECT:

PLACE:

PERSON (historical or living):

PART 4: Describe Yourself

Circle all words/phrases that apply to you:

SHY	OUTGOING
OUTDOOR TYPE	INDOOR TYPE
POSITIVE	NEGATIVE
PARTY PERSON	COUCH POTATO
HOMEBODY	LEADER
FOLLOWER	MOODY
CALM	SILLY
HAPPY	SAD
RELAXED	ENERGETIC
INTELLECTUAL	CLEVER
NEAT	MESSY
FUNNY	HONEST
SNEAKY	DISHONEST
OPEN-MINDED	JUDGMENTAL
CARING	CREATIVE
PRACTICAL	WILD
CAREFUL	WELL-LIKED
ARTISTIC	LAZY
OPINIONATED	IMAGINATIVE
REALISTIC	DRAMATIC
STREETWISE	TOLERANT
HARD-WORKING	SPONTANEOUS
STRONG	BRAVE
CURIOUS	QUIET
CHATTY	DARK
SUNNY	DISAPPOINTING
HOPEFUL	UNDERSTANDING
KIND	BORED
DIFFICULT	COMPLICATED
SWEET	POWERFUL
MACHO	ENTHUSIASTIC
GIRLY	INSECURE
LUCKY	PICKY
DISADVANTAGED	FRIENDLY
GOSSIPY	ANGRY
SECRETIVE	WISHY-WASHY
INDEPENDENT	GEEKY
WEAK	COOL
NURTURING	ANNOYING
REBELLIOUS	GOOD

PART 5: Truth/Dreams

If I die tomorrow, people will remember me as a:

One thing that really annoys me is:

My worst habit is:

I'm really scared of:

My parents think I'm:

When I grow up, I want to be*:

Superpower I'd most like to have:

The thing I'd most like to change about myself is:

My greatest talent is:

I'd most like to travel to:

Three professions I'd like to try:

The title for the story of my life would be:

* If your character is an adult, what is your character's job and does he or she enjoy it?

PLAYWRIGHT'S CHECKLIST

Does my play have:

☐ **Conflict?**

If everyone gets along, not much happens! It's important to have conflict in any play, comedy, or drama.

☐ **Character development?**

Do the characters change at all in the course of the play for better or worse? It's interesting to the audience to see some variety in character. We all act differently in different situations, so it makes sense for a character to become more complex when he or she is faced with conflicts.

☐ **Plot twists?**

What could be more exciting than being surprised by a plot twist you hadn't expected?

☐ **Believable dialogue?**

Even if the characters are strange and out-of-this-world, make sure the dialogue sounds something like the way people actually speak to one another. Any character voices you create must remain consistent throughout. For example, if a character is very intellectual and proper, having them say "I ain't gonna go" is going to seem very out of place.

☐ **A strong sense of place and time?**

Especially when you don't have a big set and costumes, it's important to make the play's setting clear.

☐ **Characters you can relate to?**

Every play has at least one character the audience can understand and sympathize with. A good way to create conflict is to put this "normal" character in the path of another character that is odd, otherworldly, or downright horrible!

SCENE ELEMENTS WORKSHEET

Answer these questions for each scene you do.

WHO: (Who are you?)

WHERE: (Where are you?)

WHEN: (Is this the past, present, or future? Day or night?)

WHY: (Why are you where you are?)

OBJECTIVE: (What do you want?)

ACTIONS: (What do you do to get what you want? For example, beg, flatter, pressure, and so on.)

CHARACTER TRAITS: (What are you like as a person?)

RELATIONSHIP: (What are your relationships to the other characters?)

OBSTACLES: (What or who stands in the way of your objective?)

EXPLORATION GAMES

Draw a picture of your character(s).

Improvise a scene before the play begins or after it ends.

Dress as your character(s) to see how it changes your behavior.

Make the scene or play into a musical or an opera.

Listen closely to everyone around you during a scene.

Try to make your acting partners respond to your behavior.

Lead with a different body part: in other words, change which part of your body enters the room first and pulls you forward when you walk. Leading with your nose can make you seem pompous, leading with the top of your head can make you seem insecure, etc.

Change the speed/rhythm at which you speak or move.

Decide who you like and who you don't like in the scene; don't be afraid to show it.

Change your volume (whisper or speak out loudly).

Make your voice higher or lower in pitch.

Notice who's taller and who's shorter than you in the scene; let this affect you.

Change your accent.

Sit down with another actor to make up your characters' past lives together.

Do an activity you think your character might do.

Do a chore around the house the way your character might do it.

Write a diary entry, a letter of complaint, or a personal ad as your character.

Come up with a gesture that your character does habitually.

THE AUTHOR

Kristen Dabrowski is an actress, writer, acting teacher, and director. She received her MFA from The Oxford School of Drama in Oxford, England. The actor's life has taken her all over the United States and England. Her other books, published by Smith and Kraus, include *111 Monologues for Middle School Actors Volume 1, The Ultimate Audition Book for Teens 3, 20 Ten-Minute Plays for Teens,* and the *Teens Speak* series. Currently, she lives in the world's smallest apartment in New York City. You can contact the author at monologue madness@yahoo.com.